THE COLORADO TRAIL **IN CRISIS**

THE COLORADO TRAIL
IN CRISIS

A Naturalist's Field Report on Climate
Change in Mountain Ecosystems

Karl Ford

UNIVERSITY PRESS OF COLORADO
Denver

© 2024 by University Press of Colorado

Published by University Press of Colorado
1580 North Logan Street, Suite 660
PMB 39883
Denver, Colorado 80203-1942

All rights reserved

 The University Press of Colorado is a proud member of the Association of University Presses.

The University Press of Colorado is a cooperative publishing enterprise supported, in part, by Adams State University, Colorado State University, Fort Lewis College, Metropolitan State University of Denver, University of Alaska Fairbanks, University of Colorado, University of Denver, University of Northern Colorado, University of Wyoming, Utah State University, and Western Colorado University.

ISBN: 978-1-64642-598-3 (hardcover)
ISBN: 978-1-64642-599-0 (paperback)
ISBN: 978-1-64642-600-3 (ebook)
https://doi.org/10.5876/9781646426003

Library of Congress Cataloging-in-Publication Data

Names: Ford, Karl L., author.
Title: Colorado mountain ecosystems in climate crisis : a field report from the Colorado Trail and other notes / Karl Ford.
Other titles: Field report from the Colorado Trail and other notes
Description: Denver : University Press of Colorado, [2024] | Includes bibliographical references and index.
Identifiers: LCCN 2024002461 (print) | LCCN 2024002462 (ebook) | ISBN 9781646425983 (hardcover) | ISBN 9781646425990 (paperback) | ISBN 9781646426003 (ebook)
Subjects: LCSH: Mountain ecology—Colorado. | Forest ecology—Colorado. | Climatic changes—Colorado. | Colorado Trail (Colo.)—Description and travel. | Colorado Trail (Colo.)—Environmental conditions.
Classification: LCC F782.R6 F67 2024 (print) | LCC F782.R6 (ebook) | DDC 577.309788—dc23/eng/20240214
LC record available at https://lccn.loc.gov/2024002461
LC ebook record available at https://lccn.loc.gov/2024002462

Cover photograph by Karl Ford

For Melissa, Ryan, Iris, and Conner
May they enjoy the serenity of the Colorado Trail

Open your eyes to the landscape. It will speak its health or sickness to you. See the wildflowers, the living forest, the dead forest, the overly dense forest, the burn scars, the rushing streams, the ebbing streams, the trout rising or not rising, the cerulean bluebird skies or smoke pall in the air; see lynx, moose, elk, or bears if you are lucky. Or not. Or maybe a wolf someday, if you are really lucky. See all of these, and behold Wakan Tanka touched by the hand of man.

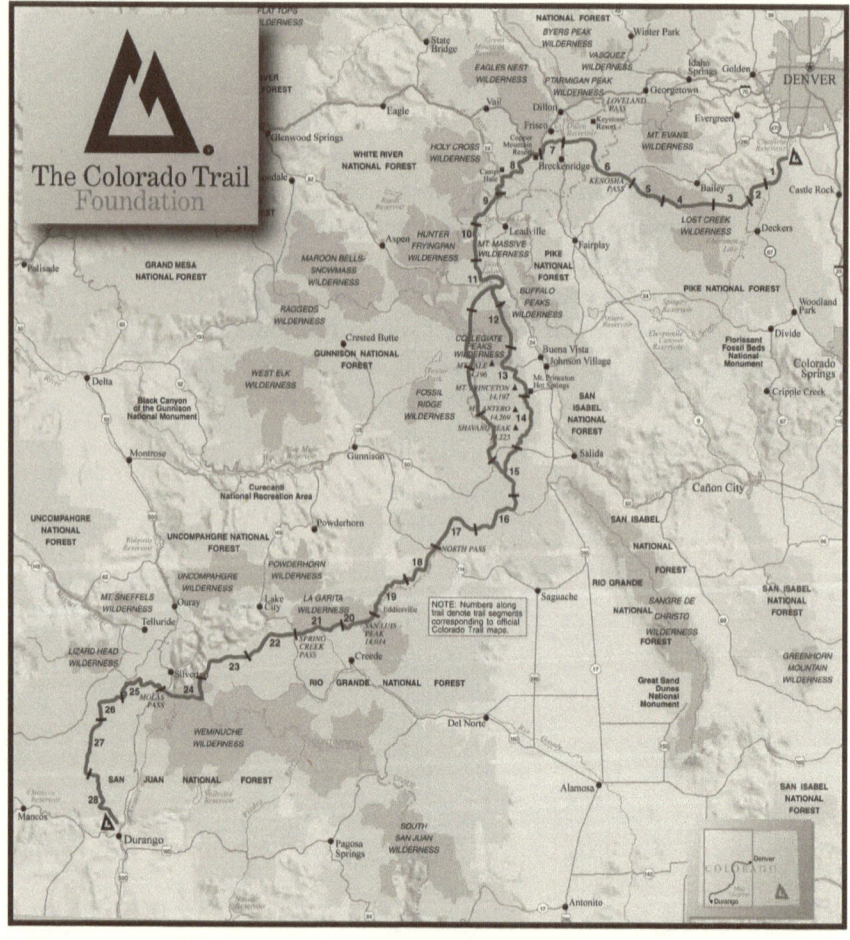

MAP 1. Map courtesy of the Colorado Trail Foundation. Numbers refer to trail segments. Wilderness areas and national forest are shown in shading.

Contents

Preface   ix

1. The Colorado Trail   3
2. Waterton to Kenosha: The Montane Forest   8
3. Kenosha to Monarch Pass: The Subalpine Zone   24
4. The New Normal of Forest Health   46
5. Our Public Lands   54
6. Monarch Pass to Creede: Subalpine and Alpine   61
7. Creede to Silverton: The Alpine Zone   90
8. Silverton to Durango: More Alpine and Living Forest   110

Epilogue: The Future of Colorado Forests   117

Acknowledgments   129
Appendix A: Leave only (Small) Footprints   131
Appendix B: Letter to Editor, Denver Post   135
References (with Some Annotations)   137
Index   147
About the Author   161

Figures follow page 60

Preface

I hope this book will help you see landscape environmental changes that are undergoing even now, in Colorado and West-wide. Colorado may not have the attention-grabbing headlines of hurricanes and massive flooding that plague millions in the East. But out West, we have our own emerging climate crisis that threatens our beloved mountain landscapes, forests, watersheds, and economy. I hope the book will inspire you to do your part in addressing climate change and protecting our precious public lands legacy. And I want you to get out and see the still-beautiful Colorado Trail.

I report here on my observations of the health of Colorado's headwater landscapes, particularly from the lens of our changing climate. Not strictly as a scientist conducting grand experiments, although I am a scientist and a naturalist, but more from observations with a scientist's eye. I will cite some facts, studies, and expert opinions, and I have tried to synthesize them with my own observations. I wrap the science into the story of my 500-mile walk in Colorado's mountain landscapes. I share some of my own perspective and context in the hope that these help to understand what I have to say in this book.

I'm not religious in practice, but with some Lakota Oglala Sioux ancestry, I have been interested in the Lakota culture and religion. I have read Black Elk, Lame Deer, and the story of White Buffalo Calf Woman and tried to distill some meaning for myself. I came to believe in a Great Spirit, called Wakan Tanka by the Lakota, the power or the sacredness that resides in everything. Every creature and object are seen as a relative, and nature is to be revered and respected. In some small way, I wanted to reconnect with my American Indian roots in the land of the Utes (hereafter, I have generally abbreviated "American Indian/s" as "Indian/s"; "Native" and "Native American," as well as specific tribal names, are used as well).

The Lakota, Ute, and other tribes still practice the *zuya*, or vision quest, that requires elements of pipe smoking, sweat lodge, fasting, isolation, prayer, and meditation. Minus the sweat lodge and pipe, I hoped my hike would be like a vision quest. I was able to isolate in natural surroundings away from distractions experienced in everyday life by choosing an area of natural beauty—the Colorado Trail. I spent time appreciating the beauty of the area and taking time to contemplate the wildlife, trees, plants, and flowers and overall health. Spending some time alone provided me with the opportunity to meditate and contemplate on life in general, the natural surroundings, and the sights and sounds of the outdoors. I did not fast, but the strenuous hiking and spartan trail food allowed for some cleansing of my body from toxins and released me from the routine of everyday life. I was not rewarded with a life-changing vision, but I became determined to tell this story.

Zen is another ancient spiritual practice that interests me. My dictionary says Zen is a state of calm attentiveness in which one's actions are guided by intuition. I can reach what I think is a Zen-like state when I am hiking. I consider being in the wilderness to be all about harmony, spiritual and physical appreciation of nature's beauty, and healthy functioning. I gravitate to Zen's respect for nature and living in harmony with the natural way of things, and all of existence. It's about understanding your place, your relationship with other living and nonliving things, and the fundamental truths of this world, impermanence, interconnectedness—all things shared with Native American spirituality.

Aldo Leopold is considered one of the founders of America's conservation movement as well as the science of wildlife management. In his acclaimed

1948 book, *A Sand County Almanac*, he declares, "The land ethic simply enlarges the boundaries of the community to include soils, waters, plants, and animals, or collectively: the land. . . . In short, a land ethic changes the role of *Homo sapiens* from conqueror of the land-community to plain member and citizen of it. It implies respect for his fellow members, and also respect for the community as such" (1966, 239).

These are principles that we can all use to improve our appreciation for all life, so it's really through understanding these truths that we can begin to cultivate that respect and appreciation for the grand order of life in the first place. Living in this way, every moment, every interaction, and everything becomes beautiful and infinitely valuable. I see significance in something as simple as a tree, a forest, a flower, or a stream as well as the whole.

Genesis 1:28 says, "And God blessed them, and God said unto them, be fruitful, and multiply, and replenish the earth, and subdue it: and have *dominion* over the fish of the sea, and over the fowl of the air, and over every living thing that moveth upon the earth." About 300 million people lived at the time of Christ; now our planet is home to 8 billion. The "multiplying" and the "dominion" have spun far out of control, and our natural planetary systems are destabilizing according to acclaimed Swedish scientist Johan Rockström et al. (2009). Many progressive religions are beginning to address protecting the planet. There is much we need to do, and, as Ben Franklin said, "God helps those that help themselves" (*Poor Richard's Almanac*, 1736). Whether you believe in God or a Great Spirit, please remember the planet in your prayers.

Fossil fuel consumption over the past century has indirectly fueled massive global population growth and a profligate American lifestyle with serious unintended consequences—among them, climate change. It has truly been the Pandora's box of modern civilization. Climate change poses an existential threat to our environment and our whole way of life. Years ago, Garrett Hardin (1968) published the theory of the "tragedy of the commons," in the prestigious journal *Science*. It is summarized as a community's loss by an individual's gain by exploiting a "commons." For example, imagine a herder adding another animal to the pasture shared by other herders, a commons. Since the pasture is limited, it can only sustain so many animals, and if each herder keeps adding animals for individual gain, the pasture is overgrazed to the point that all the animals die and the pasture is ruined. In many ways, our society is ruining our planetary commons, from overfishing and overgrazing to plastic pollution but especially by the crisis of our generation—pumping unimaginable amounts of greenhouse gases to our shared atmosphere. And, we in developed countries are the biggest climate abusers.

I hope these themes of love for nature and of identifying and correcting the course of our destabilizing planet come through in this book.

It may be premature to preside over the death of our mountain landscapes. I may be called Chicken Little from the old fable of "the sky is falling," but maybe it really is? My hike on the Colorado Trail is my humble platform for sounding the alarm to save the planet.

Open your eyes to the landscape. It will speak its health or sickness to you. See the wildflowers, the living forest, the dead forest, the overly dense forest, the burn scars, the rushing streams, the ebbing streams, the trout rising or not rising, the cerulean bluebird skies or smoke pall in the air; see lynx, moose, elk, or bears if you are lucky. Or not. Or maybe a wolf someday, if you are really lucky. See all of these, and behold Wakan Tanka touched by the hand of man.

THE COLORADO TRAIL **IN CRISIS**

1

The Colorado Trail

Why Hike the CT?

If you asked Coloradans what is our state's identity, most would say the mountains. Colorado is blessed to have the most and the highest mountains in the lower forty-eight states. We recreate here to camp, fish, hike, hunt, and ski. Besides ourselves, many tourists recreate in the mountains, and many people live and work in the mountains. We feature pictures of mountains in our postcards, paintings, photographs, and calendars. Along with our mountains is the state's biodiversity, with most of our wildlife and native plants still present in mountain ecosystems, although our biodiversity is under threat from climate change and development.

Colorado is truly blessed to have the Colorado Trail (CT). The CT is the highest long trail in the United States, averaging 10,300'. The entire trail is in the mountains. Much of the trail traces the Continental Divide, and, in fact, it shares the path with the Continental Divide Trail (CDT) for 314 mi. Depending on alternate routes, the CT spans at least 486 mi. between Waterton Canyon southwest of Denver, and Durango in southwest Colorado.

It traverses six wilderness areas and at least four roadless areas. While it traverses some of the finest scenery in the state, it also traverses some of the best summer range wildlife habitat in the state for elk, mule deer, moose, bighorn sheep, mountain goats, black bears, mountain lions, and lynx. However, most of the wildlife are difficult to see from the trail in the daytime because of the daily foot traffic on the trail.

The Colorado Trail begins at Waterton Canyon, where the South Platte River exits the mountains. Denver is located about 25 air mi. northwest. Any discussion of CT history must acknowledge respect for the Native American tribes that once inhabited and "owned" the land. Simplifying, the Ute Mountain Tribe inhabited the mountains, and the Arapaho and Northern Cheyenne Tribes inhabited the plains. The Ute territory overlapped that the plains tribes, and the Utes often warred with the other tribes over buffalo hunting and horses.

During the Gold Rush of 1858, miners established the settlement of Denver and outlying mining camps, invading Indian lands. Indians were often seen in Denver, and the whites often skirmished with them as the Indians objected to the invasion. Various treaties were made and broken by the whites. In 1864, Governor John Evans issued a proclamation "to kill and destroy, as enemies of the country . . . all hostile Indians." Colonel John Chivington then attacked the Arapaho and Cheyenne village at Sand Creek southeast of Denver. The Arapaho and Cheyenne were complying with orders by Evans to report to Fort Lyon. On a cold November 29, in a surprise attack at dawn, Chivington's troops attacked the camp, consisting of mostly women and children, and massacred about 230 Indians and mutilated their bodies. Evans and Chivington later left their posts but never were tried for atrocities. The Mountain Ute people held out a little longer in their mountain fastness, the site of today's Colorado Trail, as described in chapter 6. They lived sustainably with their environment, lessons we all can learn from.

Traveling southbound from Waterton, the trail begins in the foothills ecological zone and after ten or so miles enters the lower montane forests, where it stays for about 50 mi., then climbs into the upper montane to about Kenosha Pass. The montane is the lowest-elevation forested zone, composed of ponderosa pine and Douglas fir as the dominant tree species. After that, the CT traverses subalpine forest and long stretches of alpine tundra. In each zone, there are dominant forest species coexisting together.

Traveling southbound, the hiker gradually ascends from the foothills to the alpine, the same as moving northward in latitude by over a thousand miles. Conveniently, this book describes the dominant species of each zone and climate threats to the different forests as we ascend the landscape.

Each plant occupies an "ecological niche," a geography that has just the right temperature and moisture regime for its survival and reproduction. Different tree species and communities occupy different niches. Ponderosa pine for example, thrives in a much warmer, drier, environment than Engelmann spruce. Some transitional geographies may host mixed conifer species, where one species or another dominates depending on the climate of the last twenty to fifty years. People hike the CT to experience the mountains, wildlife, and forests, many unaware of the ecological systems around them.

The idea of the trail started with Bill Lucas. In 1973 Lucas was the regional forester for the eight-state Rocky Mountain region of the US Forest Service, which manages a third of Colorado. He initiated meetings focused on establishing the trail and the Colorado Mountain Trails Foundation (CTF). Gudrun "Gudy" Gaskill was asked to help organize the effort and became executive director. After many sputters, Gudy and the Colorado Mountain Club saw through the completion of the trail in 1987. She devoted the rest of her life to the CT, including hosting trail crews every year. She spent the whole summer cooking food and assembling supplies and visiting each crew of Colorado Trail volunteers (Colorado Trail Foundation 2008). She was in every way the mother of the Colorado Trail until she died in 2016. The trail is our lasting legacy from her. Being a Colorado Mountain Club member, I met Gudy a few times. I wish I had known her better. Today, the CT is managed by the Colorado Trail Foundation with funding from the US Forest Service and donations.

The mission of the CTF from its website is "to provide and maintain, through voluntary and public involvement, and in cooperation with the US Forest Service and federal Bureau of Land Management, a linear, non-motorized, sustainable, recreation trail between Denver and Durango. This trail will provide multi-day, inspirational, and educational values keyed to the diverse, high mountain, natural environment." Its vision is "to provide a unique, high-altitude experience to support environmental education, an avenue for healing and self-renewal, an appreciation for the value of natural systems, to encourage a cooperative effort to maintain these systems, and to promote a sense of public ownership" (n.d.).

I first hiked the Colorado Trail in segments over the years, beginning in the late 1990s and completing it in 2008. At first, I did not have any intention to complete the trail, but by 2006 I had it half done and so I decided I had to complete it. The CT was not well known back then and did not have heavy use. I hiked most days without seeing anyone. Like many hikers, I was working and could not afford to take off enough time for a through-hike, so I nibbled away at it for several years, a weekend here, a vacation week there, and so forth. I retired a few years later and hiked the three major national scenic long trails, completing the Triple Crown of hiking: the Appalachian Trail (AT), Pacific Crest Trail (PCT), and Continental Divide Trail (CDT) by 2018. I wrote about those adventures in my Kindle ebook *Triple Crown Hiking Adventures* (Ford 2021). In 2020, I decided that a redux of the Colorado Trail was closer to home and more realistic in the pandemic era.

On my first hike on the CT, I used *The Colorado Trail Databook*, a small pocketbook published by the Colorado Trail Foundation (2018). Although I teach map and compass courses, topographical maps are bulky and expensive, and on a long day I might need four to five maps and for a week, twenty maps or more. The *Databook* has sketch maps and trail descriptions and important features like water sources. That, along with the trail markings, was more than sufficient to navigate. For this trip, I still used the *Databook*, which is helpful in trip planning, but on the trail I used the FarOut phone app from faroutguides.com. It weighs nothing and has even more information and contour maps for the entire trail. I have used it on the other long trails I have hiked and rely on it. Some people question using a phone app because your batteries might get depleted or the phone lost or soaked. For the former, I carry a backup battery that can charge my phone at least once and have never had a problem in 10,000 mi. of hiking.

I found myself in my senior years wondering whether I can still hike the mountains and whether I can find peace and solitude away from the pandemic; the environmental crises; political divisiveness; and general tyranny, greed, and busyness of the world. I wanted to observe the health of the landscape in this era of climate change. And importantly, I needed to escape the war, traffic, smog, noise, politics, culture wars, electronics (mostly), bill-paying, password hell, home chores, and the whole constellation of life's cares for a while and recharge my mind and body. For me, getting into the backcountry is a constant need or refuge from the scary world.

My second hike on the CT spanned two seasons. The year 2020 had the hottest August on record for the state. In 2020, western Colorado had just completed its second-hottest summer on record. Red flag warnings and fire bans were the daily norm. A red flag warning means small fuels are less than 8 percent moisture, relative humidity less than 25 percent, and winds greater than 15 miles per hour—all dangerous conditions for wildfire—as we shall see in the next chapters.

During the winter and spring of 2021, the area was still in extreme drought. My hikes on the Pacific Crest Trail and the Continental Divide Trails took me through nearly 6,000 miles of western forests where I saw, firsthand, active wildfires, hundreds of miles of burned forests, and unburned but dead forests killed by insects. Because of these conditions and a horrific wildfire year in 2020, I needed to revisit the CT once more and report on its condition, not only as a trail but as a case study and viewing portal to the status of environmental health of mountain ecosystems in Colorado.

2

Waterton to Kenosha

The Montane Forest

Pandemic Spring

It's the late spring of 2020, the country is suffering the beginnings of the pandemic, and the West is gripped in two decades of drought. In the same way that we didn't fathom the future scope of the pandemic, most people don't understand the difference between weather and climate / climate change. Weather or climate variability means changes in climate that occur within smaller timeframes—such as a month, a season, or a year—whereas climate change is a change that occurs over a longer period of time, typically over decades or longer. It's hard for most urbanites to see the slow-motion climate crisis when they still can buy groceries, water their lawns, run air-conditioning, and drive automobiles. But ask water utilities, ski areas, farmers and wildland fire fighters, and they will express their alarm. Even the Department of Defense has identified climate change as a critical national security threat.

In an interesting twist, the pandemic lockdown kept cars off the roads and reduced our greenhouse gases (carbon dioxide and methane) and other emissions to the lowest levels in years. Temporarily—and only to be replaced by other ominous pollutants later that summer.

Setting aside worries about climate change and the pandemic, I had to escape coronavirus confinement and hit the Colorado Trail. The Waterton Canyon trailhead was closed due to COVID-19, but I could legally access it via Roxborough State Park, and with my partner Anne's help, I did. At 5,950', Roxborough was beautiful with spring flowers blooming, Gambel oaks leafing out in clean pale green leaves, and great red rocks. I climbed over Carpenter Peak exiting the park into the Pike National Forest and a pretty ponderosa pine and Colorado blue spruce forest walk led me to Waterton Canyon, where the Colorado Trail was open.

Waterton Canyon was created by the South Platte River, which originates in the Colorado high country and traverses the canyon to reach the plains. Historically, the Denver, South Park and Pacific Railroad was constructed here but was abandoned. It is known for good fishing, lots of day hikers, and the Denver water storage and treatment facilities. Bighorn sheep occur in the canyon and offer a rare opportunity for viewing at low elevation near the Denver metropolitan area. The official trailhead is at the mouth of Waterton Canyon and is flat road walking for 7 mi.

Whether you start at Waterton Canyon or Roxborough Park, the terrain is where the forests meet the plains. Forests may seem simple but are deceptively biologically complex and but a part of ecosystems. Ecosystems are geographic areas where plants, animals, and other organisms, as well as weather and landscape, work together to form a bubble of life. Ecosystems contain biotic factors, or living parts, as well as abiotic factors, or nonliving parts. We tend to identify dominant tree species, birds, and mammals in ecosystems, but hundreds of other plants, fungi, insects, and invertebrates are at work in the soil, litter, and wood, decomposing organic matter, recycling nutrients, passing water, nutrients, and carbon in symbiosis from one to another.

As you climb the mountain, it gets cooler and wetter. As we travel upward in elevation, there tend to be more precipitation and colder temperatures. For every 1,000' in elevation, the temperature drops 3–5°F. So, for example, on a given day, in Waterton Canyon at 5,500' the summer high might be 85°F, whereas at 12,500' it might be 21–35°F cooler. (Part of the attraction of hiking the mountains is to escape the hot summers at home.)

All of our mountain ecosystems are found on the CT. Very broadly speaking, they are also called "life zones" and are defined by plant and animal associations, climate conditions called an "ecological niche," as mentioned earlier, and indirectly by elevation. The Colorado Natural Heritage Program (2020) lists six alpine ecological systems; up to fourteen forest and woodland ecosystems; and one shrub, steppe, and savannah ecosystem—all found on the CT. For my purposes, I group them according to life zones used by Audrey Benedict (2008) in her *Naturalist's Guide to the Southern Rockies*.

Our lowest-elevation mountain ecosystem is the foothill zone, characterized by both shrubs and some trees in wetter areas. Waterton Canyon lies within the foothill zone. Trees need 20–25" of precipitation a year as provided in this zone. We see plains tree species such as native cottonwood and wild plum, and also montane species such as rocky mountain juniper, scrub oak, some Douglas fir, and ponderosa pine in wetter areas. The foothills zone ranges from about 5,500' to 7,500'.

Each plant occupies an ecological niche, a geography that has just the right temperature and moisture regime for its survival and reproduction. Different tree species and communities occupy different niches. Ponderosa pine, for example, thrives in a much warmer, drier environment than does Engelmann spruce. Some transitional geographies may host mixed conifer species, where one species or another dominates depending on the climate of the last twenty to fifty years. People hike the Colorado Trail to experience the mountains, wildlife, and forests, many unaware of the ecological systems around them.

Traveling uphill brings us to the montane (forested) zone, 7,500–9,000'. With 25–30" of precipitation, typical forest species are ponderosa pine, Douglas fir, aspen, mountain mahogany, and so forth. Next up in Colorado is the lodgepole pine, limber pine, and aspen zone, at 9,000'–10,000', with around 30" of precipitation per year. Lodgepole grow on dry ridges and aspen in wetter areas.

Continuing uphill, the subalpine zone ranges from 10,000' to treeline at about 11,500' and has more than 30" per year in the form of mostly snow. The subalpine contains Engelmann spruce and subalpine fir. In Colorado, spruce may be 400 or more years old. Patches of snow may linger into July and August, and trees grow slowly due to shortened growing seasons. Unlike the lower life zones, where fire-adapted species rebound in a few years, regeneration after fire in the subalpine is slow and requires sustained wet years. Valley floors are filled with wet meadows and willows.

The uppermost life zone is the alpine tundra, where trees don't grow (except sparsely as very stunted and gnarled shrubs) and the vegetation consists of grasses and forbs. Many areas are bare rock with maybe a few miniature species growing in crevices. The harsh climate precludes trees or larger shrubs, and wildflowers can be spectacular.

The preceding description is a gross simplification because there are many exceptions and some species cross life zones depending on location east or west of the Continental Divide, slope aspect, soils, and moisture. For example, sagebrush appears up to 10,000' on the Western Slope in the big parklands like the Cochetopa Valley but is uncommon on the eastern slope. There are also variances to these general rules based on forest succession. A complicated and controversial concept, *succession* is a term basically used to describe the sequence of pioneering species that first occur after a disturbance such as fire or logging. In succession, later species dominate as soil moisture and shade become more suitable. It's important to note the more complex the ecosystem, the more resilient it is to threats like wildfire, insect pests, and climate change.

As an example of the complexity, the work of scientists like Suzanne Simard has shown that trees communicate with one another via roots and fungal mycorrhizal networks. Her book *Finding the Mother Tree* (2021) tells that, with shocking similarity to humans, elder "mother" trees can discern their young, share resources with them if they are sick, and alert them to insect pests and disease so they can mobilize defenses. Understory plants like birch and alder can even share nutrients and water with seedlings of fir even while shading them from the drying effects of the sun.

Simard reports that clear-cut logging practices in British Columbia entailed stripping all native plants from newly planted seedlings. The resulting damage to soil and vegetation destroyed mycorrhizal fungal networks and nurse shrubs. Loggers prefer large, old-growth trees to harvest because they are commercially more valuable. But removing larger, healthy, reproducing trees takes away the elders and leaves young trees to fend for themselves. Like humans and overpopulation, what trees can't do by themselves is thin overly dense stands. In a healthy forest, fire and insect pests maintain stable densities, matching the available sunshine, moisture, and nutrients. Older trees are necessary for forest health. But our changing climate is challenging forests' resilience to exaggerated fire and pests.

The fungus *Rhizopogon* is a common mycorrhizal fungus for ponderosa and lodgepole pine. It forms "false truffles" underground that Abert squirrels treasure. According to Gabi Morey, education outreach director, San Juan Mountains Association, the squirrels actually help the ponderosa pine trees, in addition to using them. Ponderosa pine trees have a mutualistic relationship with mycorrhizal fungi, found in the soil. The fungi extend the reach of the tree's roots, helping it get to more water, phosphate, nitrogen, and other nutrients, while the tree provides the fungi with carbohydrates. From late spring to early fall, the squirrels eat the "fruiting body" of the ectomycorrhizal fungi—the part that shows up aboveground for part of the year. This mushroom has spores throughout it, which the fungi use to reproduce. When eaten, the spores survive through the digestive tract of the squirrel, coming out in its scat, and get spread throughout the ponderosa pine forest, especially those trees where the squirrels like to hang out. This is an amazing trifecta of a mutualistic relationship—among the Abert squirrels, ponderosa pine trees, and ectomycorrhizal fungi.

I often see live pine twigs clipped off and lying on the ground in ponderosa pine forests. Abert squirrels gnaw off the ends of the branches, letting the pine needle ends fall to the ground. They retain the remainder of the branch, removing the outer bark and eating the inner bark.

From about mile 10 to mile 60, the CT traverses montane forests at lower elevations, from about 6,000' to 10,000'; it tends to be snow free by the late spring and is normally quite hot and dry in the summer. This forest is principally second-growth ponderosa pine and Douglas fir with a few aspens. The small Gambel or scrub oak species occur at lowest elevations in the first 30 mi. near Waterton and again near Durango. Their bright green leaves provide a scenic contrast with the darker conifers, and many wildlife species including bears and deer love their acorns in the fall and winter.

Because of the pandemic, hardly anyone was out on the trail. I was just planning an out-and-back hike but managed to get 25 mi. in on the CT, climbing to 7,500' in the ponderosa pine forest followed by a steep descent to the South Platte River. Much of the early portions of the CT travel through the ponderosa pine or montane forest. In these areas, I observed a very dense forest with many downed trees mixed with prevalent Douglas fir trees. This is a problem.

Fire on the Mountain

According to recent work by Forest Service researcher Mike Battaglia and coauthors (2018), management practices since the late nineteenth century, including harvesting and fire exclusion, have altered the structure of ponderosa-pine-dominated forests in Colorado. Widespread harvesting and human burning during the settlement era (second half of the nineteenth century) consisted of heavy selective logging of the larger trees that opened up stands, creating higher light levels, a wetter climate, and bare mineral soil suitable for new establishment of conifer seedlings. Throughout the West, many of today's dense stands originated after nineteenth-century logging-created regeneration. Logging often transforms lower-density stands dominated by large-diameter trees into dense stands of small-diameter trees 120 years later. These structural changes have contributed to uncharacteristic wildfire behavior and effects (Veblen, Romme, and Regan 2012; Funk 2014).

Battaglia used dendrochronology (the study of tree rings) to reconstruct presettlement-era forest structure for 170 plots in montane ponderosa-pine-dominated forests of the Colorado and Wyoming Front Range. Historical reconstructions were compared with current conditions. In lower montane forests, historical basal (trunk) area per acre was three times less, and the density per acre was five times less than current density. So, there were more open forests. Most of the plots showed evidence of old logging. Thus, the current greater density is a combination of human disturbance and fire exclusion. I found tree densities in this study to be consistent with what I see in the montane forests I hike. These younger, lower montane forests are much too crowded, creating vulnerability to pests, drought, disease, and wildfire.

Across the montane zone, pine are decreasing due to infilling of the more fire-vulnerable Douglas fir, a bad sign for wildfire. Fir trees have more lower branches that serve as ladder fuels. Montane forests of ponderosa pine and Douglas fir in Colorado today are characterized by dense stands of trees due to a variety of causes including fire exclusion, regeneration pulses after past harvesting, and regrowth after widespread burning during the nineteenth century.

Although the causes of high-stand densities vary from site to site, there is no doubt that these forests are now vulnerable to large, high-severity burning. Despite these areas being resilient to nineteenth-century and earlier episodes of burning, observations of recent fires indicate that many areas are *not* regenerating to forests of ponderosa pine and Douglas fir under current climate. A new study led by the University of Colorado Boulder also finds that large parts of the Southern Rocky Mountains ecoregion will become unsuitable for ponderosa pine and Douglas fir regrowth as the climate continues to warm. Lead author Kyle Rodman and his team (2020) found a stark timeline, with very little regrowth after the 2000 Walker Ranch Fire near Boulder. Two years later in 2002, the Hayman Fire burned more than 138,000 acres near the trail and was the state's largest wildfire for many years. The year 2002, Rodman says, "was one of the driest years we've had in the past century or more. So, any seedlings that might have established right after the fire, there's a good chance they would have been cooked in that drought." I take Wilderness Trekking School groups to Walker Ranch and have hiked the Hayman and other burns. I can vouch that little forest growth is occurring.

Studies by Rodman and others (Coop et al. 2020; Rodman 2022) found that Front Range ponderosa pine forests are unlikely to be able to regenerate under a future warmer climate. According to climate modeling, by 2051, under the moderate emissions scenario, less than 18 percent of Douglas fir and ponderosa pine forests will likely recover if burned. Under the higher-emission scenario, that number dips to 6.3 percent for Douglas fir and 3.5 percent for pine forests. Threats to ponderosa pine are threats to its forest wildlife, including Abert squirrels, grouse, mule deer, and bighorn sheep. The twigs and needles are browsed by mule deer, sheep, and elk. The inner bark of young trees is eaten by bears and by porcupines in winter.

Scientists call larger wildfires; insect attacks; even human activities like logging, grazing, and other surface changes *disturbance regimes*. A disturbance regime is a general term that describes the temporal and spatial characteristics of a disturbance agent and its impact of that agent on the landscape. More specifically, a disturbance regime is the cumulative effects of multiple disturbance events over space and time and may change the type (state) of vegetation.

Forest resilience to climate change is a global concern given the effects of increased disturbance activity, warming temperatures, and increased moisture stress on plants. Camille Stevens-Rumann (2018) used a multiregional dataset across fifty-two wildfires from the US Rocky Mountains to ask if and how changing climate over the last several decades impacted postfire tree regeneration, a key indicator of forest resilience. Like the work by others, results highlighted significant decreases in tree regeneration in the twenty-first century. Annual moisture deficits were significantly greater 2000–2015 as compared to 1985–1999, suggesting increasingly unfavorable postfire growing conditions, corresponding to significantly lower seedling densities and increased regeneration failure. Dry forests that already occur at the edge of their climatic tolerance are most prone to conversion to nonforests after wildfires.

When a disturbance regime makes a wholesale change of vegetation type, say from forest to shrubland, scientists call it a *change of state*, meaning major, permanent ecological change. In the past, we have seen major changes in state from grassland to shrubland caused by overgrazing in the Southwest. What Rodman and Tom Veblen are seeing is a state change caused by wildfire, but the underlying cause is climate change. It's too hot and dry for tree seedlings to survive, and drought-tolerant shrubs like mountain mahogany prevail.

In an interview with Dr. Veblen—a University of Colorado Distinguished Professor and expert on forest mortality, bark beetles, and wildfire—I asked about natural regeneration and reforestation by artificial planting. Veblen agreed that most of the fires in the montane ponderosa pine forests are not reforesting naturally. While there has been less research in the subalpine forests, Veblen believes similar trends will hold true for reforestation of subalpine spruce and subalpine fir forests along the Western Slope of the Colorado Trail. He said reforestation efforts in the montane may need to consider species better adapted to warm, dry conditions such as pinyon pine and juniper. Reforestation in the subalpine should consider more heat-tolerant limber pine, Douglas fir, and even Gambel oak. Planting should be focused on wetter, cooler sites, where chances of success are greatest.

He told me that the greatest threat to natural regeneration is to have wildfire follow a beetle kill because any living seed source is incinerated. Where beetles kill nearly all the large cone-producing Engelmann spruce, seed availability for regeneration following a fire in the same stand may impede postfire regeneration. Spruce seeds are slightly wind dispersed, so there will be some regeneration up to several hundred feet.

On the other hand, pines have large seeds, which are less dispersed by wind and are limited to sites more immediate to the seed trees. Only Clark's nutcracker and squirrels can move seeds, and neither can eke out a living in a dead forest. We know that individual Clark's nutcrackers cache tens of thousands of seeds (often more than 30,000 each) and can relocate them as long as nine months after the original burial. And Colorado nurseries currently cannot provide many seedlings for reforestation. Veblen also told me that contrary to popular opinion, beetle-killed subalpine forests don't pose a wildfire threat any greater than a living forest when drought conditions are present. Both wildfires and large-scale beetle outbreaks are driven primarily by warm, dry climatic conditions rather than one being the cause of the other.

Buffalo Creek and Hayman

After climbing 2,000', at about mile 13, I reached a high point with long views to the south and west. The light-colored barren burn scar of the Hayman Fire dominated the view south for as far as I could see. The Buffalo Creek Fire Burn scar is visible to the west. I then descended to the South Platte River. The South Platte is a major water supply stream for the Denver area and is dammed at Strontia Springs a few miles downstream. This area was the site of one of Colorado's water wars where the Denver Water Board wanted to dam the river at a different location and allow the South Platte and North Fork Valleys to fill at Two Forks, creating a much larger reservoir. But environmentalists and, ultimately, the Environmental Protection Agency (EPA) halted the project in favor of other alternatives including water conservation. Today, the river was busy with people fishing and day-hiking, so I watered up and hiked a few more miles and camped on dry hills above the river.

The next morning, I packed up early and headed west through the 1996 Buffalo Creek Burn. There were few, if any, conifers growing in the burn scar, twenty-five years later. There were many wildflowers and shrubs such as mountain mahogany, mountain ninebark, raspberries, and young aspen. In the area, I could also see burn scars from the 2000 Hi Meadow Fire, the 2012 North Fork Fire, and, most notably, the 2002 Hayman Fire. All of these fires were in ponderosa pine forests. For many years, Hayman had the record for the largest area burn in the state. But that was about to change in 2020, as I will discuss later.

The Hayman Fire started on June 8, 2002, 35 mi. northwest of Colorado Springs, Colorado, and 22 mi. southwest of Denver, Colorado, and was, for eighteen years, the largest wildfire in the state's recorded history, at over 138,114 acres. The fast-moving Hayman Fire caused nearly $40 million in firefighting costs, burned 133 homes, and forced the evacuation of 5,340 people. The National Interagency Fire Center defines *megafires* as a large fire exceeding 100,000 acres. In contrast to ordinary wildfires, megafires have the potential to permanently transform the landscape (National Geographic Society Resource Library 2023).

According to Tania Schoennagel, Thomas Veblen, and William Romme (2004), at Hayman in the spring of 2002 there was low snowpack as well as low humidity. Measurements of large-fuel moisture in mid- to low-elevation forests of the Southern Rockies were among the driest in the previous few decades, dipping as low as 3 percent. Small fuels must have approached zero moisture. It was the classic tinderbox. The size and severity of the Hayman Fire can largely be explained by the extreme fire activity during two separate periods associated with sustained, exceptionally dry, forceful winds (Graham 2003). First, on June 9, the fire grew by 45 percent; later, on June 18, it traveled 5 mi. along its southeastern flank. During these two periods, mean relative humidity dipped below 8 percent, and maximum wind gusts reached 84 mi. per hour.

Smoke could be seen and smelled across the state from Vail to Burlington, and from Broomfield to Walsenburg. The Hayman Fire burned from June 8, 2002, until it was classified as contained on July 18, 2002. The cause of the wildfire was found to be arson.

Andrew Chiodi, Brian E. Potter, and Narasimhan K. Larkin (2021) have reported a 50 percent decrease in a metric called nighttime vapor pressure deficit (VPD) over the Rocky Mountain foothills since 1981. I recently learned VPD is an air dryness metric preferred by scientists over relative humidity. Whereas relative humidity is a measure of the saturation of the air with moisture at a given temperature, VPD is the difference between saturation and the current amount of moisture in the air, in terms of pressure. Nighttime VPD is widely believed to account for extreme wildfire behavior.

Fire ecologists rate wildfires in terms of severity. Low severity means damage to soils and vegetation is low; this type of fire is ideal in clearing ground fuels, preserving larger trees, and making the forest more fire-resilient. Moderate- and high-severity fires burn very hot and may eliminate most-to-all vegetation and seriously damage the soil's ability to hold water and allow germination. Fire severity can destroy ectomycorrhizal fungi in the soil and helps explain poor plant and forest regeneration, even in the presence of seeds because high-severity burned soils are sterilized and become hydrophobic, shedding water.

Each forest community has a unique fire regime and even for the same broadly defined forest type, such as ponderosa pine community type, there is much variability in the fire regime associated with topographic position (e.g., north vs. south-facing slopes, ridge tops vs. valley bottoms, steep slopes vs. rolling topography). Regime refers to average fire return intervals in years to the same place, and burn severity is most typically measured as the percentage of trees killed.

Tom said prior to modern fire suppression, lower montane forests of ponderosa pine were characterized by relatively frequent fires with return intervals often of twenty or fewer years that typically burned at low severity, killing only tree seedlings and saplings but not mature trees. In contrast, subalpine forests of lodgepole pine, Engelmann spruce, and subalpine fir typically burned at long intervals measured in centuries but at high severities, killing most trees in "stand-replacing" events. While these two ends of a continuum are widely applied to describe frequent, low-severity fire versus infrequent stand-replacing fire regimes, there is a large part of the landscape that does not fit easily into these two categories—an intermediate upper montane zone is often described as a "mixed-severity fire regime."

For example, the upper montane forests of ponderosa pine, Douglas fir, and other species in the Colorado Front Range naturally had a mixed-severity fire regime of both moderately frequent surface fires of low severity and infrequent higher-severity fires killing not all but significant numbers of large trees over many acres. Public understanding of the natural role of fires in Colorado forests has often been challenged by the difficulty researchers have in communicating the importance of the heterogeneity of past fire occurrence—fires varied widely in their behavior and occurrence across the landscape and also over time in association with climate trends and weather events.

Tom said lodgepole and spruce forests don't burn often, but when they do, it is usually with high severity. A study by Kimberley Davis and sixty-two coauthors (2023) found the probability of conifer recruitment in the San Juan Mountains of southwest Colorado to be 0.76–0.88 after low-severity fire but only 0.18–0.36 after high-severity fire, and climate warming and drying were found to be the key limiting factors. Ominously, the Hayman Fire was rated high severity even though it was in mostly ponderosa pine and the ladder fuel, Douglas fir.

Back at Hayman, twenty-plus years later, researchers were disturbed about the lack of reforestation. "What we're seeing is a very large high-severity burn patch, where the vast majority of the trees have died," says Marin Chambers, with the Colorado Forest Restoration Institute at Colorado State University (2020). These 18 sq. mi. burned hot and fast in a single day, driven by how dense the forest was because of past fire suppression, high winds, and extreme drought. Now, two decades later, something you would normally see after a wildfire is missing: new trees.

"Some regeneration may be occurring, but certainly not enough to recreate a forest in the near term," Chambers (Chambers, Colorado Forest Restoration Institute, and Colorado State University 2020) says. She and her colleagues have found that forests are struggling to grow back some of the state's most iconic species, like ponderosa pine and Douglas fir. High-severity fires leave behind massive burn areas with almost nothing alive. And any seedlings simply can't survive in the increased heat and drought brought on by climate change.

"Imagine being a ponderosa pine seed trying to grow out here," Chambers says. "It's a pretty intense environment."

If there is forest regeneration, Chambers says, it happens in bands along the forest edge, where surviving trees can still drop their seeds. But, she notes, even that isn't happening at lower elevations, where it's hotter and drier. She is not sure this area of the Hayman Fire will ever reforest.

If there was any doubt that the increasing wildfire activity is due to climate change, John Abatzoglou and A. Park Williams (2016) found that increased forest fire activity across the western US in recent decades has likely been enabled by a number of factors, including the legacy of fire suppression and human settlement, natural climate variability, and human-caused climate change. They use modeled climate projections to estimate the contribution of anthropogenic climate change to observed increases in eight fuel metrics and forest fire areas across the western United States. They estimate that human-caused climate change contributed to an additional 4.2 million ha (1 ha = about 2.5 acres) of forest fire area during 1984–2015, nearly doubling the forest fire area expected in its absence. Natural climate variability will continue to alternate between modulating and compounding anthropogenic increases in fuel aridity, but anthropogenic climate change has emerged as a driver of increased forest fire activity and should continue to do so while fuels are not limiting.

Wildfire and climate change were not in the public's collective consciousness in the spring of 2020. Everyone was locked down, wearing masks, and hoping it would soon be over. This was to change later in the year.

I continued my CT spring hike through the 1996 Buffalo Creek Burn. It was dry, sun exposed, and warmed quickly. This section has no water and the forest has not regenerated at all, although there are plenty of shrubs and wildflowers. I was seeing a state change, like the Hayman Fire or Walker Fire converting the forest to shrubland. In a rare bit of unburned timber, I passed a small logging operation—wondering if it was legal. The loggers were not salvaging burned timber but were cutting live trees. I hiked to the fire station, where I got water and hiked on to the Buffalo Creek Road at mile 27, where I turned around for home. I saw only a handful of people on the trail the whole way. It was great to get out for a few days, and the weather was perfect.

Lost Creek Wilderness

In the early summer of 2018, I hiked the next section from the Buffalo Creek Road to Kenosha Pass with Colorado Mountain Club friends Anne, Kasey, Alison, and Jim. Anne joined for the east leg of the hike past Little Scraggy Mountain and over major rock outcrops. We were a little tired on our third day, but she was fresh. She surprised us with major trail magic! The next morning, Anne was leading hiking slowly and I said she could speed up. Boy, did we regret that, as we chased her all day! This area was dry also, with few water sources. Mountain biking loops are extensive in this area and make use of sections of the Colorado Trail. I have taken the Colorado Mountain Club Wilderness School on off-trail graduation hikes in this area.

On the trail, we met a grandmother and her grandson hiking the CT with a llama. Grandma chose renting a llama over carrying heavy packs, and she had no experience with llamas or backpacking. Credit to her for tackling an adventure they will never forget! I hope to hike with my granddaughter in a few years when she is old enough.

We passed Buffalo Creek and campground and got water at an oasis area on the creek. We camped near the Rolling Rock trailhead and in the growing dusk practiced hanging bear bags—always good for a laugh as long as the rope and rock don't bean you. Most hikers tie a small bag with a rock in it to a rope and throw it over a high limb. This is not as easy as it sounds and usually takes multiple tries. When the rope drops over the intended branch, the backswing seems to come right for your head. In my experience, most hikers don't bother hanging their food, but the possibility of a hungry bear slashing your tent at night is not worth the risk. I use an Ursack made of Kevlar that doesn't have to be hung and tie it to a tree well away from my tent. Tying the Ursack to a tree keeps a bear from carrying it away.

From miles 42 to 49 and miles 57 to 64, the trail traverses the beautiful Lost Creek Wilderness and Kenosha Mountains. Known for its long meadows, polished granite domes, spires, and knobs, it resembles Yosemite Valley on a more intimate scale. We had easy hiking through the majestic, peaceful meadows alongside the North Fork of Lost Creek. The North Fork joins Lost Creek and flows through the wilderness, disappearing underground more times than you can count on a map or in the field. The creek itself is mostly inaccessible. I have hiked into the Lost Creek Wilderness many times and I am always surprised by something new, like gnarled, dead, red, old bristlecone pines, delicate lady's slipper orchids, the disappearing creek, the old shaft house, the beaver ponds with brook trout, and, in recent years, even moose.

Because of its proximity to the Denver area, according to wilderness advocate and historian Mark Pearson, Lost Creek received more comments favoring its designation in 1972 than any other in the country. But final designation had to wait until 1980, with an addition in 1993 (Fielder and Pearson 2002). Getting wilderness preserved is a generational thing. Conservationists have been at it since 1964, when the Wilderness Act was signed. Our children will hopefully carry the torch for future wilderness protection in the decades to come.

A few years ago, I led a climate education overnight backpack in the Lost Creek Wilderness. We hiked in about 8 mi. to Refrigerator Gulch, aptly named because it is a cold canyon. I and some colleagues from Wild Connections (see discussion later in chapter) were working on a mapping exercise to locate places in central Colorado that were "cold air pools," or

CAPS. I brought a temperature data logger, and we measured temperatures throughout our hike. Sure enough, the ridges were warmer than the canyon bottoms, by as much as 5–10°F. These CAPS tend to carry streams and are wetter. They are potential refugia for native plants and wildlife that may be able to survive the warming temperature and drought of climate change. When linked together, they may serve as climate corridors for native plants and migrate northward or uphill to reach their changing ecological niche of temperature and moisture.

Back on the CT, we climbed briefly into subalpine forest, at 10,500', where I had seen the hillside studded with mushrooms in an earlier fall trip. The trail passes through the northern parkland of the wilderness, called Long Gulch, with long, willow-filled meadows (called carrs by biologists) teeming with beaver, brook trout, and probably cutthroat trout. We descended into a lovely Long Gulch along the North Fork of Lost Creek, where we were treated to nearly 6 mi. of easy walking along an open stream valley full of willows and beaver ponds.

Beavers are an important tool to help combat climate change. By damming streams and flooding ponds, they can control flooding, remove sediment, recharge groundwater, and encourage riparian vegetation. Stream corridors are CAPS and important climate refugia and migration corridors for plants and animals adapting to climate change. Beavers are also a keystone species: their hydrologic engineering creates a biodiverse wetland habitat for hundreds of other species, from moose to songbirds. Beaver wetlands also create plant and animal refugia from wildfire and help sequester carbon in pond sediment. They also can be natural fire breaks that help contain wildfire.

We camped near Black Creek in the deep forest. Pine squirrels were abundant and noisy. These squirrels are responsible for the pine-cone middens you see in the forest. A midden is a deep pile of pine-cone fragments and pine seed caches. Like Abert squirrels, they also love mushrooms. I saw several forest birds—downy woodpeckers, nuthatches, chickadees, and brown creepers—all of which seek insects in the tree bark,

The next day, we continued west past the Long Gulch trailhead at mile 57. Here, near the Rock Creek trailhead, in 2017 with Wild Connections volunteers I helped close a portion jeep road for the Forest Service on a volunteer project. They had ripped up the old road, and we raked, seeded, and mulched it. The restoration was well along when I passed by. Wild

Connections has performed many such restoration projects for the Forest Service and Bureau of Land Management (BLM) lands on the eastern side of the Continental Divide.

I served as a board member of Wild Connections (wildconnections.org), a conservation nonprofit that advocates for wildlife and wilderness in the central Colorado mountains, including this part of the CT. In a multiyear project, we mapped climate refugia and corridors where wildlife and plants can persist and migrate as the climate changes. As I mentioned before, these areas tend to be along stream corridors and canyons that incidentally are important wildlife, native plant, and high-biodiversity areas. Wild Connections advocates for greater protection of these areas from mining, drilling, and motorized uses to preserve these sanctuaries for biodiversity into the future. The Pike–San Isabel National Forest is due to revise its forest plan, and we hope our work will be used to protect these critical areas. Now, and in the coming years, we will see how the plant and animal communities are changing in the face of climate change.

We climbed gently into aspen-covered hillsides and sagebrush meadows with long smoky views into South Park, eventually reaching Kenosha Pass at mile 72, the end of our hike. We could see smoke mushroom clouds from the Weston Pass wildfire over in the Mosquito Range on the southwest side of South Park. It was just another wildfire yet was a foreshadowing of things to come.

3

Kenosha to Monarch Pass

The Subalpine Zone

Grasshopper Joins the Hike

My hiking friend Grasshopper from Portland met me in July 2020 to continue my hike from Kenosha Pass to Monarch Pass on the CT. I think he got his trail name from his long, skinny legs. Those legs help him hike a lot faster than I can with my short legs. We have hiked over a thousand miles together on long trails and summited Kilimanjaro together. Like me, he is a senior citizen type but in amazing shape, the peloton king of the northwest. We share common interests in the environment and politics. Grasshopper retired from the computer hardware industry. He is into brain science and is educating me on it.

Back when we hiked the John Muir Trail together, Grasshopper taught himself Mandarin Chinese (no small feat) and would listen to teaching recordings with earbuds while on the trail. Once, on the CDT, near Old Faithful, we were headed into town and gave a lift to three young hotel workers who were chattering in Mandarin in the back seat. Grasshopper was

https://doi.org/10.5876/9781646426003.c003

driving and entered the conversation, flabbergasting them! Happened again at Twin Lakes while we were resupplying and some Chinese tourists were there. He also has a trove of jokes to keep us chuckling. Like me, he is an ultralight hiker, which helps immeasurably on those long-mile days. Like me, he is a grandfather who helps watch his grandchildren.

We had chosen mid-July to allow snow to melt and mosquitoes to thin out. I hoped to still see lots of wildflowers, but I knew the early wildflowers that follow snowmelt would be gone. The downside of this timing is that it put us in the monsoon season and that we could expect daily rain.

Kenosha Pass was used by the Utes and early explorer John C. Frémont in the 1840s. In 1870, the South Park and Pacific Railroad pushed tracks over Kenosha Pass. In 1937, the tracks were removed and replaced by the highway. I have hiked along what is left of the old railway where it occurs off the highway. The tracks are gone, but it is a pleasant, evenly graded walk with cuts and fills, obviously an old railroad even though trees are invading.

The next sections would lead us into the subalpine forest and alpine zones from 10,000' to over 12,000'. This forest consists mainly of lodgepole pine, Engelmann spruce, and subalpine fir with smaller pockets of aspen, limber pine, and bristlecone pine. Once again wildfires were burning in the western states, and we were concerned about wildfire and smoke on our hike. We could not know how awful this summer would be for wildfire.

Grasshopper flew into Denver, and we put him up for a night to begin to acclimatize. If you are coming from sea level, it may take a week or more to adjust to the Colorado Trail altitudes. Anne took us to Kenosha Pass, and we got dropped off in the early evening. The original plan was to hike in a few miles and set up camp, but feeling the excitement of the new hike, we went on into the dusk through aspen groves, views of South Park, and easy hiking to Jefferson Creek. Arriving in the dark, we found most campsites were taken but went off-trail a little way and found a campsite near the rushing creek for the night.

The previous January, I had hiked and snowshoed this section with a friend, wanting to get a sense of the snowpack conditions. It was early winter, and there were about 24" of snow in the forest. On the exposed west- and south-facing hillsides, the snow had melted off. Snowpack is very sensitive to slope aspect and terrain. North-facing slopes hold the snow the longest—hence most ski areas have north-facing terrain. On the high peaks above treeline, it mostly blows away, evaporates, or settles into the valleys, especially in the forest where trees trap it from the wind. Here, snow is shaded and persists for the spring thaw and melt.

Colorado has fourteen remnant, named glaciers—all in the Front Range, most significantly in Rocky Mountain National Park. And they are very small. The total area of all the mapped snow and ice bodies in Colorado is only about three sq. mi. Most glaciers and snowfields in Colorado occur in east-to-north-facing cirques at high elevations near the ridge crests. These locations favor snow accumulation from avalanches and windblown snow in the winter, and are well shaded from summer sun (Cox 2021). They are melting fast and will be gone in my children's lifetime.

Colorado has many more rock glaciers, perhaps over 3,500, often hiding in plain sight (Rick 2022). When you think of a mountain glacier, you might imagine a large mass of white or blue ice, hanging in a cirque or flowing into a U-shaped valley. However, glaciers can be made of rock as well, or rather a combination of rock and ice. These *rock glaciers* can form when an ice glacier is buried with rock debris from surrounding slopes, or through a gradual process of many years of snowmelt freezing within a rocky slope until it starts to move downhill. Rock glaciers suggest permafrost.

We think of permafrost melting as happening in the Arctic when, in fact, it is common in the alpine areas of Colorado above treeline in wind-scoured areas that remain snow free in winter. On flatter areas in summer, thawed depressions filled with water are widespread in permafrost areas, especially in those underlain with perennially frozen silt. They may occur on hillsides or even on hilltops and are good indicators of ice-rich permafrost. In some areas, soil slumping from thawing (solifluction) is another indicator, especially along roadcuts or even the trail. I have hiked on the tundra with untold numbers of small, shallow ponds and hummocks that are likely permafrost. From San Luis Peak past and beyond Molas Pass, hikers will pass by permafrost areas and may not even notice. So what?

Climate warming is capable of accelerating permafrost melting and the decomposition of previously frozen carbon. John Knowles and others (2019) studied an area on Niwot Ridge on a snow-scoured alpine tundra meadow in Colorado, where solifluction lobes are associated with discontinuous permafrost. On average, via microbial soil respiration, the ecosystem was a net annual source of about 232 g of carbon per square meter to the atmosphere.

Given that alpine soils with permafrost occupy 3.6 million sq. km of land area worldwide, this scenario has global implications for climate change.

In the subalpine, snowpack melts preferentially under trees as the melting snow drips off the tree branches. The dripping melts the snowpack faster under trees than between trees, creating extreme hummocks difficult to hike through. April is generally the month of greatest snowfall, but warming temperatures tend to melt at a rate that exceeds accumulation. The snowpack gets denser and contains more water as it warms.

Sublimation takes its toll on the snowpack, and snow can evaporate without even melting to liquid water. Hiking in April and May usually involves bothersome postholing or late season snowshoeing. Not until early July is the trail usually clear of snow enough for travel at higher elevations. Intrepid and prepared backcountry travelers can traverse the trail in the spring, but snowshoes, microspikes, ice axes, and astute knowledge of avalanche avoidance are required. Some winter backcountry skiers travel with an emergency beacon, show shovel, and probe along with equally prepared companions, in case of avalanche.

In winter, most wildlife at this elevation have hibernated or migrated to warmer climates, even lower elevations. Only moose, mountain goats, ptarmigan, pine martens, squirrels, an occasional porcupine, coyote, fox, bobcat, and raven are about in this area, and they are few and hard to see. Moose feed on willows and conifer needles in the winter; mountain goats use their powerful shoulders to sweep aside snow to get at last summer's grasses. Squirrels seek their nut caches under the snow while keeping wary of pine martens. Secretive snowshoe hare and lynx are also about in the San Juan Mountains, playing their survival games of hide-and-seek. Foxes, coyotes, wolves, and bobcats have such excellent hearing they can hear rodents under the snow. They will stalk voles and gophers in *subnivean* (Latin for "under snow") zones, pounce high in the air and dive into the snow at the precise location where the rodent is, and capture and eat it.

I like to look for tracks, but often they are so imperfect from melting and blowing snow, they are hard to identify. All wildlife will hunker down and shelter in the worst storms, either under the snow or in dense forest where the winds are less powerful. At lower elevations, deer and elk slowly starve, eating whatever low nutrition browse they can find. It never fails to amaze me that the larger mammal females can carry their young through extended winter starvation, still manage to deliver healthy young, and are able to nurse them with sparse feed in the early spring. Fortunately, the spring plant growth is highly nutritious and helps quickly revive their condition. Hungry bears begin to emerge at lower elevations looking for carrion that they can smell miles away. On the Western Slope, sage grouse begin dancing on their sagebrush leks, which are special clearings where males display themselves for females.

By May, aspens begin to unfurl their tender light green leaves, shrubs are budding out, sap begins to flow in the conifers, and early wildflowers like globeflowers and glacier lilies welcome back the hiker with their splash of color, even against the receding snow drifts and last summer's dull brown grasses. Migratory birds begin to appear, courting and nesting in the short growing season. Deer and elk follow the "green up," moving either northward or uphill to the most nutritious early growth. All the wildlife get serious about delivering and caring for their young, even as vagrant storms occasionally set the calendar back into winter.

Hummingbirds appear, sometimes while snow still lies on the ground and insects are few. They are so small and their metabolism is so incredibly fast that they need to refuel about every ten minutes. Each day they consume 50 percent of their body weight just to maintain their normal weight. Hummingbirds burn thousands of calories per day—at least as much as humans do. When it is still cold and lacking nectar, they seek out sweet sap from trees and early insects to survive. All this palate of life starts at the lowest elevations in April and moves upward, week by week, until even the tundra becomes alive by early June.

The snowmelt that is so critical to us all starts in April on warm, sunny days, with snow dripping off branches and rocks, saturating the soil, running off into the smallest creeks, with hundreds of little creeklets gurgling and flowing into streams. The snowpack consolidates and compacts with some ground showing through. By May, the streams become bank-full and rush to the rivers. The peak runoff is normally in late May to early June, and backcountry travel can be dangerous if stream fords are required. I recall solo-hiking on the remote CDT in June in the Wind River Range of Wyoming and fording ten or more large streams a day. Crossing the streams was much more dangerous than the grizzly bears in the area. Climate change is causing the peak runoff period to occur two-to-four weeks earlier than thirty years ago, which is a problem for our mountain ecosystems and humans alike.

Early runoff leads to early drying of the mountain landscape. In summer, smaller tributary creeks dry up, fish lose habitat, soils dry out, and riparian vegetation struggles for survival. With warming, forests dry out in drought and lose humidity and moisture in fuels, making forests more flammable and contributing to longer fire seasons, not to mention stressing plants into survival mode. Without adequate water, for example, conifers can't combat bark beetle attacks by flushing sap through their point of entry. For humans, early runoff is harder to capture in reservoirs, and much of the water is lost downstream. In the arid West, higher-elevation reservoirs are needed to provide water via gravity flow for agriculture and urban use, including hydroelectric power, a renewable energy.

It was a thankfully cool morning as we climbed 11,875' Georgia Pass enjoying fine but slightly smoky views of towering Mount Guyot followed by a nice tundra walk. In 1880, Georgia Pass was a wagon road over the Continental Divide used by miners bound for gold in the Breckenridge area. This summer, central Colorado was in a major drought; fires were burning in California and Oregon, and we were concerned about wildfire. The tundra had dried and the wildflower show had passed, but all was serene and peaceful. We descended down into the Swan River drainage, crossing its tributaries several times, and saw some mule deer. We camped near a creek at a small meadow and listened to the gurgling creek flow. The following morning, we descended gradually through dry lodgepole pine forests passing a turnoff to the Continental Divide Trail. These forests have stunted trees, often only 4–5" in trunk diameter and growing so densely that no understory can survive.

The Colorado Trail and CDT are the same southbound for the next several hundred miles. The CDT angles northward over Grays Peak and on along the Continental Divide through the state, while the CT heads west and south. North of I-70, especially in the Arapaho-Roosevelt National Forest, mountain pine beetles have attacked lodgepole pine on a landscape basis, affecting millions of acres. Since lodgepole tends to form a monoculture that dominates all other tree species, in many areas all of the trees are dead. Fortunately, the CT has not been too impacted by pine beetles and the forest looks reasonably healthy here, although the trees are even aged and too dense. The forest is vulnerable to wildfire and beetles.

As mentioned earlier, ponderosa pine dominates the montane (lower-elevation forest). Mid-elevations along the CT are home to more lodgepole pine east of the Divide and more mixed conifer and aspen west of the Divide on the CT. Lodgepole pines are drought hardy, and their serotinous cones can seed profusely after fire or harvest to create extremely dense stands of stunted trees, often subject to windthrow and pine beetle mortality. The subalpine life zone of the upper elevations on both sides of the Divide contains limber pine, subalpine fir, Engelmann spruce, and bristlecone pine.

One of my favorite subalpine wildflowers is fireweed, a tall pink showy plant with many bright pink flowers. They are a fire-successional plant, growing often in the blackened, ash-covered soils after a recent fire, providing stark counterpoint to the blackened landscape. They will grow in other areas too, especially disturbed areas like roadsides.

Bristlecone pines are gnarled, red-barked, and five-needled; they are found well spaced at timberline commonly on dry slopes. Slopes are typically steep (20–35°) and aspects are usually south- or west-facing, although they may occur on any aspect with well-drained soil. Soils in these areas are only inches deep, very cold year-round, and acidic. Unsurprisingly, bristlecone pines are slow growing, but among the oldest organisms on the planet, excluding aspen clones and possibly mycorrhizal fungi. They can reach several thousand years old. Some trees look dead but have a few live branches. Dead snags may persist for a hundred years in the dry, cold climate until wind finally blows them over.

The day grew warm, but we hiked through lodgepole forest and lush meadows to Highway 9. Anne met us at Gold Hill with a food resupply and drove us into Frisco, where we masked up for a cold brew and dinner. This Blue River Valley is still recovering from stream dredging performed by miners in the 1860s, which left great piles of cobbles and no vegetation. A boat-like dredge was floated and pumped stream gravels through screens and collected gold nuggets, leaving the stream a ruin. You can still see an old dredge in Breckenridge. We took a short swim in Dillon Reservoir and enjoyed a peaceful campsite for the night.

Beautiful Wild

Anne drove us back to the trail the next day and hiked partway into the Tenmile Range with us. She then said goodbye and returned to her car. We hiked on into a large clear-cut right on the Colorado Trail. Dubbed the Ophir Mountain Forest Health and Fuels Reduction Project, it consists of 1,500 clear-cut acres in the White River National Forest southwest of Frisco. The Forest Service defends clear-cuts in the name of fuels reduction and wildfire prevention, although there is little scientific evidence that thinning alone or clear-cuts reduce wildfires. There is evidence however, that trees can reforest better in restrained thinning projects that leave mother trees, mycorrhizal networks, and understory behind. Despite no homes or structures to defend, the trees were cut, chipped, and trucked 70 mi. to the Eagle Valley Clean Energy biomass facility in Gypsum (Schlossberg 2014).

We continued up a stiff climb to the top of the Tenmile Range at about 12,500', where we could see the top of Breckenridge ski lifts and all over the Blue River Valley; massive Dillon Reservoir; and the towering 14ers, Grays Peak, and Torreys Peak, east across the valley, not far from where we were a few days ago. I saw a few patches of snow, tinged pink. Watermelon snow—also called snow algae, pink snow, red snow, or blood snow—is a phenomenon caused by *Chlamydomonas nivalis*, a species of green algae. The algae contains a secondary red carotenoid pigment (astaxanthin) in addition to chlorophyll. Unlike most species of freshwater algae, this species appears to be cryophilic (cold loving) and thrives in freezing water.

Colorado is fortunate to have a wealth of high mountains, fifty-eight over 14,000' alone. These peaks are magnets to peak-baggers from around the world. In 2021, over 303,000 hiker days were estimated by the Colorado Fourteeners Initiative, and trailheads can be jammed on summer weekends, especially on the Front Range. There are several 14ers near the Colorado Trail. I have hiked many of them and lots of 13ers too, of which Colorado has 637. Some peak-baggers have done them all and many more. These days, I prefer long-distance hiking for the solitude and nature fix.

Some of these high peaks are home to mountain goats. Standing about 3–4' at the shoulder, and big shoulders the billy goats truly have, they are powerful beasts. They are also fairly uncommon, found only above treeline. You might get lucky and see them on a side hike to a 14er like Mount Elbert, Mount Massive, Shavano Peak, or San Luis Peak. In summer, they shed their all white, heavy winter coats and great clots of fur droop off their bodies, giving them a shaggy appearance. Most scientists agree the goats are not native to Colorado but were introduced from the northwest states in 1947 and have spread throughout the high peaks. They are the only large mammal to weather the severe winters at altitude. Hikers and tourists can see them on top of 14ers Grays Peak and the formerly named Mount Evans. Of course, Governor Evans was the instigator of the Sand Creek Massacre. In 2023, it was proposed that the name of the mountain be changed to Mount Blue Sky, a recommendation of and out of respect for the Native tribes.

In the 1960s, the town of Dillon was relocated from the Blue River Valley by the Denver Water Board and the Dillon Reservoir constructed to store water for a transmountain diversion to water-hungry Denver. After enjoying the view of Dillon Reservoir, we made a steep descent from the ridge across avalanche debris slopes, which brought us down to Tenmile Creek and Copper Mountain.

Tenmile Creek has also been impacted by mining. In my lifetime, various mining companies, including Amax, mined molybdenum at the head of the Tenmile Creek Valley, carving out the mountain at 10,000' and filling the valley with mine tailings. Only in the last decade or so has any land reclamation been done and a water treatment plant installed. The creek is in better shape these days and is also part of Denver's water supply as it flows into Lake Dillon. We crossed the creek on a new bridge and hiked on a few miles through ski slopes at Copper Mountain and found a nice campsite in the pines for the evening.

The next morning, we hiked out and made a short detour into the Copper Mountain ski area and grabbed a coffee and roll at Starbucks! The ski resort lies in another mountain valley that has been paved over and filled with hotels and condos. In a hurry to leave it behind, we continued on west picking up Guller Creek and ascending this lovely, verdant valley. A passing hiker warned us of moose ahead, so we kept our eyes peeled but did not see any. Moose were extirpated by meat hunters in Colorado but reintroduced in 1978, and seeing them is always a thrill. Moose are dangerous to hikers if approached too closely. They are becoming a hazard for humans, encroaching on urban areas, causing car accidents, and occasionally trampling people or dogs who get too near. Most people are tolerant of the majestic moose and don't complain too much. People like to see deer, elk, and moose but not bears, wolves, or mountain lions, when actually the former are more dangerous. Deer injure and kill more people in America than carnivores.

Moose ferment woody forage in their stomachs, generating heat. That, their large body size, black coat, and lack of ability to perspire make them very sensitive to heat. They do quite well in wintry conditions, feeding on willows. In summer, they love aquatic vegetation and water in general. They may be seen in ponds submerging their heads below water and feeding on aquatic vegetation. This cools them and keeps insects away.

While moose populations appear to be expanding in Colorado, several climate change factors may threaten Colorado moose numbers in the future. They are increasing temperatures and two consequences of those increases: changes in forest species they rely on and increasing parasites, especially winter ticks. Thousands of ticks can be on one moose, causing anemia and loss of fur and contribute to declining numbers. In Wyoming, moose are declining and are currently being studied for this reason. Moose are perfectly adapted to cold but may do poorly in the warmer weather expected in Colorado's future.

The hike climbed onto the Elk Ridge of the Gore Range. At treeline is Janet's Cabin, a winter hut open for backcountry skiers and snowshoers and operated by the Tenth Mountain Division Hut Association. I remember passing it on my first hike, surprised to see a nice cabin in a roadless area. The Hut Association maintains a network of twelve backcountry huts, several of which I have had the privilege of bunking at. We passed by and climbed on up through drizzling rain over Searle Pass at 12,034' and beyond for three fine miles on top of the Divide to Kokomo Pass. We enjoyed a quick break before descending into the east fork of the Eagle River. Most of our hiking is at the top of the watersheds, and when I say "river" it really means a creek you could jump across. The country here is wetter and greener closer to the Divide.

The trail then descended through beautiful Engelmann spruces and subalpine firs that gave way to lodgepole pines and aspens at lower elevations. It then headed westerly, past a great waterfall on Cataract Creek, where Grasshopper took a fully clothed shower in the icy water. Not as daring, I took a soapless sponge bath. We continued on the open flats and camped at old Camp Hale, site of the winter training for the Tenth Mountain Division of the US Army, which fought in the Alps in World War II. As the camp was dismantled in 1963, only a few of the old bunkers still remain for hikers to explore, although signs warn of possible unexploded ordnance in the area.

After my hike, in 2022, President Biden designated the Camp Hale–Continental Divide National Monument to protect this historic site and adjacent wilderness. It encompasses 58,034 acres around Camp Hale and the Tenmile Range. The Tenth Mountain Division that trained at Camp Hale helped lead our nation to victory in World War II, then went on to create the outdoor industry as we know it today. The National Monument designation ensures Camp Hale's historic preservation, secures existing recreational opportunities, and protects natural resources.

The next day we had an easy walk through lodgepole forest and meadow and joined an old narrow-gauge railroad bed. The Denver and Rio Grande Western Railroad constructed this rail line over Tennessee Pass in 1881 as part of its extension to the Aspen area in order to beat the Colorado Midland Railway's standard-gauge route to Aspen's rich mining area. There are some old charcoal/coke ovens near the trail at the pass. Coke ovens were common in the Leadville area during the mining boom and were used to fire the town's mining smelters. Coal was burned in the ovens with limited air to drive off moisture and volatile gases. The resulting coke was a superior fuel for the smelters. We arrived at the Tennessee Pass trailhead, where we had some trail magic and chatted with day hikers and a couple finishing the trail at Tennessee Pass. We have entered the headwaters of the Arkansas River.

A recent plan by the state to kill black bears and mountain lions at the Upper Arkansas River and other areas of Colorado was intended to artificially boost the mule deer population for hunters, where habitat had been degraded by oil and gas drilling. But overwhelming scientific evidence shows that killing native carnivores does not boost prey populations. The killing plans were hatched and approved by Colorado Parks and Wildlife in 2016 and funded by the US Fish and Wildlife Service in 2017, despite overwhelming public opposition and over the objection of leading conservation biologists' voices. Their plan was halted in District Court.

Our next leg took us west into the Holy Cross Wilderness. One of the wetter areas of Colorado's central mountains, the Holy Cross Wilderness is named for the 14er Mount of the Holy Cross. The mountain can be seen from vantage points on the CT. In 1873, the cross's historic beauty was made famous worldwide by photographer William Henry Jackson, who doctored his photos to enhance the cross-shaped snow-filled couloirs on its eastern face. Jackson was part of the famous Ferdinand Hayden's 1873 US Geological

Survey topographic expedition; Jackson summited on August 22. Hayden is also known for his Yellowstone expeditions in 1871 and 1872.

Most of the wilderness lies in high-altitude lakes and streams west of the Divide, where they capture more snow and rain from westerly storms. The wilderness has many high peaks, streams, lakes, and waterfalls, and the trail passes several of them in its short but scenic traverse from mile 150 to 156. We camped near an unnamed lake and walked down to the lake at dusk to soak in the peaceful evening. Wetlands and streams provide critical habitat for Colorado's 400+ species of birds. According to Colorado Parks and Wildlife (n.d.), wetlands comprise less than 2 percent of Colorado's landscape but provide benefits to over 75 percent of the species in the state, including waterfowl and several declining species! Since the beginning of major settlement activities, Colorado has lost half of its wetlands. By virtue of their position in the landscape, wetlands perform several functions valuable to wildlife and society, including feeding, provision of habitat for resting and rearing, movement corridors, groundwater recharge, stream bank stabilization, and sediment and nutrient removal. I looked for boreal toads, a Colorado endangered species, once common but now very rare and limited to higher aquatic habitats and wet meadows. The chytrid fungus is suspected to be the primary reason, but the toads rely on ponds that may be susceptible to drought and climate change. I did not have rubber boots with me, so I did not see any.

Like Holy Cross, most of Colorado's wilderness areas are at high elevation where deep winter snows and melting snowpack are like a great water fountain in the sky for the whole state and downstream states. The snowpack normally melts slowly, releasing peak flows to stream and rivers in early July, but north-facing protected snowfields and groundwater contribute healthy flows year-round. As the climate changes, snowpack is now more meager and melts faster. In Colorado, the snowpack is melting a month earlier than the norm. This change leaves the landscape drier throughout the entire summer and fall, creating dangerous wildfire conditions and drought-stressed forests.

Because of its water resources, wilderness designation was complicated by the Homestake Water Project, which diverts west-slope water underground through tunnels and into the Turquoise Lake reservoir in the Arkansas River Watershed. Language from its wilderness designation allows for future water development, and Eagle County and conservationists continue court battles

High Peaks Wilderness

We hiked into the subalpine, where we encountered wet, complex terrain with many streams, creeks, and ponds, ultimately descending down to the busy Turquoise Lake trailhead. As a boy, I used to camp in this area with my parents and explore the Carlton Tunnel and Hagerman Tunnel area. Here, the Colorado Midland Railway crossed the Divide at Hagerman Tunnel, 11,985'. To gain the elevation, the longest and most spectacular wooden trestle (bridge) in Colorado was built in 1887. The Hagerman Trestle was 1,084' long, 84' high, and 200° in curvature. The trestle was still standing when I was a boy but was later dismantled.

I remember the deep valley that the Bureau of Reclamation dammed in 1967 to store transmountain water from the Western Slope for the cities of Aurora, Colorado Springs, and Pueblo. That water storage is Turquoise Lake. On my first trek through here twenty years ago, it was June and I had to abort because of heavy snows in the alpine area. I was solo and not equipped to cross the deep snow. Ice does not even melt out of Turquoise Lake until late May, and the high lakes may not follow for another month.

Grasshopper and I continued south climbing into the Mount Massive Wilderness. Colorado's second-tallest, and arguably its largest, mountain is Mount Massive, at 14,421'. The mountain has five summits, all above 14,000', and a summit ridge over 3 mi. long, resulting in more area above 14,000' than any other mountain in the forty-eight contiguous states. The area has over 30 sq. mi. of terrain above timberline. Named for its massive mountain, the Mount Massive Wilderness graces about 10 mi. of the CT from mile 160 to 169.5. There is a turnoff to the Mount Massive side trail, and some CT hikers make the 3,500' climb. I had previously climbed Massive, and so I passed on the summit.

The towering Continental Divide creates a rain shadow from the prevailing storms from the west. Most of the trail in this area lies east of the Divide and below treeline as it contours around the east flank of Massive in a second-growth, dry lodgepole pine forest with a few aspen groves in wetter areas.

Much of this forest was clear-cut in the 1880s for mining and shoring the underground mine works in the nearby Leadville area. Leadville is near the headwaters of the Arkansas River, a major tributary of the Mississippi River. With its colorful mining history, Leadville was the second-largest city in Colorado in the late nineteenth century. It is also touted as the highest-elevation town in America, at 10,200'. In the modern era, many efforts (including my own via BLM) have been made to remediate acid mine drainage and mine waste from the Leadville area. Many CT hikers visit Leadville for rest days and to experience its "old mining west" history and culture. We enjoyed expansive views from the trail over the Arkansas River Valley ranches and towns for many miles.

Grasshopper and I exited the wilderness area and hiked down to Halfmoon Creek trailhead, where we had a fine camp in the ponderosa pines. In the morning, we hiked out early, as usual, and continued south past the Mount Elbert trail junction. At 14,440', it is the highest in the state and second highest (to Mount Whitney) in the lower forty-eight states. Climbing 14ers has become a passion for many; Elbert sees 20,000–25,000 people per year in all seasons, more each year. It is typical of the overcrowding of our recreation areas. I had already climbed it, so we decided to continue on the big traverse along the east side of Elbert. We passed several creeks in the lodgepole forest and another trail junction to Mount Elbert and more fine aspen forests, finally arriving in Twin Lakes Village.

Situated near Twin Lakes and on the Independence Pass Road, Twin Lakes village is a picturesque perfect little trail town. It features old cabins and is very small, but you can get your resupply box or buy some trail food; there are a couple of restaurants plus some B&Bs and cabins for rent (make a reservation), and a small historical museum. Nearby is the Mount Elbert Pumped Storage hydroelectric plant at the man-made Twin Lakes, doing its part to reduce greenhouse gases. Anne met us at Twin Lakes and took us into Leadville for a *nero* (a partial hike day), where we masked up for a great dinner at the Treeline Restaurant. What a find!

In the summer of 2020, many conservatives grew impatient with wearing masks and turned masks into a political issue with talk about "you can't muzzle my children," blah, blah. The racially motivated killings of Black people that spurred protests and contributed to the growth of the Black Lives Matter movement added to the political divide that grew and festered throughout the year.

Collegiate West Traverse

The next day, Anne returned us to Twin Lakes and we said goodbye. Colorado Trail hikers enjoying this area must choose either the Collegiate Peaks East (73 miles) or Collegiate Peaks West (80 miles) route. I have done this section south from Twin Lakes three times, once on the east and twice on the west. The east curves around the lakes for several miles of hot, exposed hiking along the road and sagebrush, and ascends past Mount Yale and Mount Princeton, both 14ers I have climbed. Instead, we cut cross-country south across the open Valley of Lake Creek to return to the trail, since we were intending to take the more scenic and higher Collegiate Peaks West route. We crossed several braids of the creek at knee-high water and navigated directly to the trail junction we wanted. I think the CT doesn't cross here, because it is a seasonal or flood pool, a high-water area of the lake. The official west CT trailhead is up valley, where one big bridge is located.

At this point, hikers have to tackle Hope (I hope I make it) Pass, one of the most strenuous in the state, rising 3,250' over about four mi. But it is a beautiful hike along rushing Willis Creek and alpine terrain topping out at about 12,500'. The summit views to the south were of a baker's dozen of hulking 14ers and high 13ers. It was a little hazy from wildfire smoke but very impressive. I rested near a cairn with a pole and prayer flags draped over it. Just to the west is Hope Mountain, a near-14er. We descended down Sheep Creek through aspens into the Clear Creek drainage, where we crossed Clear Creek near the ghost town of Rockdale and camped nearby. A couple of other CT hikers joined us for the evening, which was cool and drizzly. The next morning, I captured a photo of a hazy pink-red sunrise.

Grasshopper and I hiked out up the South Fork of Clear Creek climbing back into the alpine with miles-long willow carrs (wet meadows), expecting to see moose. To our left was the towering Huron Peak, 14,006'. We entered the Collegiate Peaks Wilderness at mile 198. Nestled within the Sawatch Range, the Collegiate Peaks is arguably the highest-elevation wilderness in the Lower 48. It is home to eight 14ers and is heavily visited by climbers and hikers alike. It is so named because at least four peaks are named after universities (Columbia, Harvard, Oxford, Yale) by or for explorers and graduates of these institutions. (Mount Princeton, named for the university, lies just outside the wilderness.) There are many other high peaks in the wilderness, sculpted and carved by glaciers with cirques, deep valleys, and glacial moraines. Hikers are treated to magnificent views everywhere in the wilderness. Hikers must expect big ups and downs in this vertical country.

The Colorado Trail website claims an average trail elevation of 10,300'. Treeline (timberline) in Colorado is around 11,500', depending on slope aspect and latitude. I don't know what percent of the CT is above treeline, but it is probably nearly 50 percent overall and in some segments in the central and southern portions, more like 80 percent. It is truly a high-altitude hike with everchanging long views of Colorado's mountains. Our next stretch was a ten-mile alpine traverse. We hiked all day through the alpine and camped just beneath timberline a couple of miles below Lake Ann. I pitched my tent on a little knoll overlooking the stream.

The next morning took us up to achingly beautiful Lake Ann, a beautiful gem in a high cirque. We passed it early and watched it sparkle in the morning sun as we ascended Lake Ann Pass, 12,588'. Just below the summit is a snow cornice overhang. In early season, hikers must find a way to scramble around it, but now it was early August, and we had no trouble. Just to the east are the Three Apostles and Ice Mountain, all high 13ers.

The descent is beautiful and idyllic for several miles, then the trail leaves the wilderness and enters a jeep track/trail over a jumbly hill and down to join a vast willow carr meadow at Texas Creek. East of here is where those Collegiate Peak 14ers are concentrated. The next day we forded cold Texas Creek and climbed back into the wilderness under Mount Yale, 14,196', where we camped high near Cottonwood Pass. This area was lush and wet with recent rain, but water sources were surprisingly hard to find. Other hikers reported moose, but we saw none.

Cottonwood Pass is a recently paved high-altitude road over 12,126', one of the highest paved roads in the country. We crossed it by 6 a.m. and continued south for a very long 14 mi. alpine traverse that averages over 12,500'. This is among the most beautiful and most hazardous segments for hikers who must contend with severe monsoonal thunder and lightning storms that occur almost daily around midday. During midsummer, moisture moves northwesterly from the Pacific Ocean into southwest Colorado. The monsoon forms when the land warms up at a different rate than the Pacific Ocean does, causing the wind direction to shift and allowing moisture to travel north from Mexico. The North American Monsoon is a pattern of increased thunderstorms and rainfall over large areas of the southwestern United States and northwestern Mexico, typically occurring between July and mid-September. During the monsoon, thunderstorms are fueled by daytime heating and buildup during the afternoon to early evening.

With our good planning and early start, we were able to complete the traverse in the morning hours before weather came in. I wasn't so lucky the last time I hiked it, as poor planning put us here in the afternoon. Lightning storms came in, and we cowered off the ridgetops and waited it out as the storm and lightning lashed all around us.

Near the end of the traverse is the east portal of the old abandoned Alpine Tunnel, the highest railroad tunnel in the country. When I was a boy, my dad took my brother and me up the approach to the west side of the tunnel in his 2WD truck. It was a ledge drive with palisades above and below. We met a big boulder in the one-lane narrow road and could not pass. It was terrifying watching Dad grinding through a ten-point turn to turn the truck around. Equally terrifying was managing two-way traffic with jeeps coming up as we headed down.

A short side-hike takes one to the closed portal, but the CT continues on the flat old South Park and Pacific Railroad bed to the ghost town of Hancock on Chalk Creek. Down the road from here is the gem of Mount Princeton Hot Springs, where many a CT hiker has rested and cleansed the trail grime away. We did not partake on this trip, but I have been there many times and will go again. I noticed some new summer homes being built on old mining claims. A nasty three-mile walk up a rocky jeep road took forever, but the CT became a trail again in the high alpine passing Hancock Lakes and over pretty Chalk Creek Pass, 12,146'.

We descended into the Middle Fork of the South Arkansas River in an afternoon storm. Fortunately, we had timed it to be sheltered from lightning in the forest. A long descent dotted with wildflowers down the Middle Fork took us to the lowest point since Twin Lakes, to about 10,500'.

In the early evening, we continued up to Boss Lake on one of the steepest sections on the CT. It was cool but humid from the rain, and we sweated our way up. Parts of this trail were in terrible shape, and we could see where some new trail was being built thanks to the Colorado Trail Foundation volunteers. We found a pleasant camp overlooking the lake. This lake is actually a high-altitude reservoir serving the Upper Arkansas Valley. I watched trout rising in the calm lake in the evening. It was a very peaceful camp.

The next morning was our last on the trail for 2020. We climbed above pretty Hunt Lake to Monarch Crest, at 12,472'. The next alpine traverse along the Divide would stay above 12,000' for seven miles, where we passed interpretive signs showing how prehistoric Indians conducted game drives on the Divide funneling elk and bighorn sheep into stone corrals where they killed them. Nearby Shavano and Tabeguache Peaks are 14ers named after Ute chieftains. The Monarch Crest traverse ended with a descent through the summertime ugly of Monarch Ski area onto Monarch Pass at Highway 50. Thankful for a safe and relatively smokeless hike, we had a light lunch at the café and piled into Grasshopper's car for the long trip home.

Reentry into society is always a bit of a challenge. Cars seem to drive faster, there is more noise, more bills to pay, things to fix, traffic to contend with, jobs to do, relationships to rekindle, passwords to remember, and the overwhelming, never-ending politics and news cycle. Back at home, my metabolism still cranked up, I tended to eat too much for the slowed level of activity. It took weeks before I returned to normal. In a few months though, I was planning the next trip. Having hiked over 10,000 mi., I sometimes wonder what is my normal—in town or on the trail? But I know I will always be but a visitor in the wilderness.

Colorado Burning

Later that summer of 2020, Colorado's forests suffered a truly catastrophic wildfire season. Our attention turned from the pandemic to fears of megafire. In October, most of our statewide fuels were down to less than 5 percent moisture, with red flag warnings. On October 21, due to wildfire, the Arapaho-Roosevelt National Forest closed access to its lands in five Front Range counties. Only heavy snows saved Colorado that year. That year, the Cameron Peak, East Troublesome, and Pine Gulch Fires assumed first, second, and third places in largest megafires in recorded state history (Hayman is now fourth). Nearly 700,000 acres and many homes and structures in Colorado forests burned in 2020—by far the largest total in state recorded history. For perspective, the 1960s through the 1990s saw less than 20,000 acres burned per year, whereas the 2000s and 2010s saw 85,000 and 100,000 acres burned per year, respectively (National Interagency Fire Center n.d.). Untold thousands of migratory birds died from the smoke. With but one respite, all summer and fall, the Front Range was besieged with smoke, oppressive heat, and murky skies. It was the same throughout the West.

We can't afford more bird losses. We have lost 3 billion migratory birds since 1970, or 29 percent of all birds, according to an article published in *Science* (Rosenberg 2019), the most prestigious science journal in America. Drought, wildfire, and the unpredictable weather of a September 2020 snowstorm after record-breaking heat—all related to climate change—appear to be a factor in mortality of Colorado's bird populations, according to the authors. Most of the dead birds were insectivores—insect eaters that appear to be starving. The brown-capped rosy finch uses alpine habitat almost exclusively in Colorado mountains, where it feeds on insects trapped in snowfields and glaciers. Its numbers have declined by 95 percent; such a steep decline may get the species classified as threatened. In 2018, Wild Connections and the Colorado Bird Observatory (now Bird Conservancy of the Rockies) banded rosy finches in the Tarryall Mountains near the CT. The white-crowned sparrow, another insectivorous mountain species of the tundra, has also suffered serious declines. I did see a few of these birds on my hike, but they used to be very common. The main hypothesis for their decline is that drought has reduced the number of insects available to the birds combined with migrations through areas made dangerous by climate-related events.

The National Audubon Society (2023) modeled birds vulnerable to climate change using habitat maps and global climate models. Their maps show near total loss of habitat at 2°C warming (where we are now) for the brown-capped rosy finch and at 3°C for sixty-two other bird species in Colorado rated as highly vulnerable, including these two species and many more! (One °C equals about 1.8° F.)

Birds are not the only flighted vertebrates at risk with climate change in the Colorado mountains. Many of the eighteen species of bats found in Colorado are found in the mountains even up to treeline. Some migrate and some hibernate for the winter, but Rick Adams and Mark Hayes (2018) have found that warm/dry conditions such as we have had in the recent twenty-year drought favor a 4:1 sex ratio for males, compared to the ratios in more normal climate conditions. This finding could threaten bat reproduction and numbers as the climate continues to warm.

Forests and tundra ecosystems that have evolved over millennia are dealing with changes that may affect us for generations to come. To us it is a gradual, insidious change that not enough Coloradans notice nor understand. We have air-conditioning and the ability to turn on tap water whenever needed. Not so for our mountain ecosystems. To the forest, the change is occurring far more rapidly than older changes in climate such as ice age melting that took place over a thousand years. Forests now have only decades to adapt to warming, wildfire, insects, and drought, and adaptation will be beyond the capability of most tree species. Wildfire, insect forest mortality, and climate change are inseparably linked. While patchy, smaller forest fires are good for forest health, clearing out fuels and dead trees, the Forest Service's successful Smoky the Bear campaign suppressed most wildfires starting in 1944. Seventy years of logging of older trees, aggressive fire suppression combined with more recent warming, and insects have left our forests full of dead fuel.

While fire suppression policy has been effective at suppressing fires in the subalpine zone, the impact of fuels has so far not been significant because fuel quantity does not limit fire in spruce-fir forests. Historically, fire has been limited by climate in the subalpine zone due to monsoon rains and snow. But the climate is changing, and the subalpine is increasingly more vulnerable.

All of our large fires have occurred in the twenty-first century. Coloradans remember Spring Creek—2018, Black Forest—2013, Waldo Canyon—2012, Hayman—2002. Plus, the terrible megafires of 2020 that burned 700,000 acres. By the middle of the century, megafires are expected to triple in frequency (Iglesias, Balch, and Travis 2022). At 700,000 acres/year, this could mean 7 million acres / decade; 3.1 million acres have already burned since 2001. With 24 million acres in Colorado forests, this burn rate may not be sustainable. Our children may well see a transformation of forests that evolved over 10,000 years.

It is well established that changing climate is the major cause of megafires. And, while wildfire may be the proximate cause of some forest mortality, changing climate is a major factor in forest mortality even in unburned areas. In mid-October 2020, 90 percent of the state was in severe or greater drought and 59 percent in extreme or exceptional drought. This was the driest year since 2012 and was the second warmest and driest in recorded history, according to the Colorado Climate Center (n.d.). Robert Andrus and coauthors (2021) have shown a strong relationship between higher rates of tree mortality and warmer, drier summer climate conditions, implying that climate warming will continue to increase background mortality rates in subalpine forests. A related factor is the rise of mortality from bark beetle infestation that has killed or impacted over 21 percent of our forests and contributed to dry fuels. New studies are showing beetle populations are erupting with warming.

As the landscape warms and dries, and wildfire and insect pests claim the forests, there are hidden places on the landscape that will stay cooler and wetter—in valleys, canyons, and riparian areas. *Riparian* means wetland vegetation associated with flowing streams. These areas tend to be the most biodiverse and shelter many species of plants, fish, crustaceans, insects, reptiles, and amphibians, birds, and mammals. There is an urgent need to identify these places in our forests that must be protected to enable our ecosystems to persist or migrate. These refugia may one day serve as seeds, in a literal and figurative sense, to restore ecosystems hanging in the balance.

Contrary to popular opinion, Veblen told me, megafires are not strictly new but have burned historically but infrequently, according to tree-ring data back to the 1600s, coincident with megadrought. The West has been gripped in a West-wide drought situation for years and is unlikely to improve in the near future, scientists say. Late spring of 2021 looked to extend the *megadrought* that researchers have found to be gripping the region mostly unabated since 2000. The difference this time is the drought is largely human induced. Work by A. Park Williams and Ben Cook (2020) and A. P. Williams and Benjamin (2022) suggest the West is locked into the worst megadrought in 1,200 years. The region might have been in a state of drought regardless, "but it's really climate change that pushed this event to be one of the worst in 500 years," says Ben Cook, a climate scientist at Columbia's Lamont Doherty Earth Observatory.

Tom Veblen told me that even in the absence of fire, regeneration of the subalpine zone has been shown to depend on infrequent years of moist/cool conditions. Studies of fires in the San Juan Mountains show very poor postfire regeneration under the warmer climate of the twenty-first century. At the same time, death of adult spruce-fir trees is increasing even without any bark beetles or fire. These studies can be taken as "early warnings" of the likelihood that following future fire, there will not be much conifer regeneration.

Spruce do not regenerate well in open, beetle-killed forests and burn scars, especially during drought. According to the US Forest Service's (n.d.a), 40 to 60 percent of full shade is most favorable for Engelmann spruce seedling establishment at high elevations. Light intensity and solar radiation are high at elevations and latitudes where spruce grow in the central and southern Rocky Mountains, and seedlings do not establish readily in the open. Spruce establish and survive better in low-light intensities than lodgepole pine, Douglas fir, and aspen.

Engelmann spruce are restricted to cold, humid habitats because of their low tolerance to high temperature and drought. They need an average of 0.4" of precipitation per week. Solar radiation at high elevations heats soil surfaces to 150°F or more and increases water losses from both seedlings and soil by transpiration and evaporation. Because of its slow initial root penetration and extreme sensitivity to heat in the young, succulent stage, drought and heat girdling kill many first-year spruce seedlings. Drought losses can continue to be significant during the first five years of seedling development, especially during prolonged summer dry periods. All of these factors contribute to poor spruce regeneration.

In my hike, I never made a campfire even though I enjoy them. Fire bans were in place, and even if they were not, I don't make campfires in the backcountry. From a Leave No Trace (LNT) standpoint, they are unsightly, unnatural scars that gather ash and trash. In fact, I have often cleaned campfire rings and hauled out others' trash. Also, as a long-distance hiker, in camp I am too tired to gather firewood and build a fire then properly extinguish it. Most important, from a wildfire standpoint, fires are just too risky for our wilderness and roadless areas in this era of drought. Too many people are not sufficiently experienced or careful with fire and putting out campfires completely. I would like to see campfires actively discouraged or prohibited on the CT.

4

The New Normal of Forest Health

Primed to Burn

I have said my hike was to be a viewing portal into the environmental health of our forests. During the summer of 2020, drought conditions were extreme in Colorado, recording the second-driest year ever. As I have mentioned earlier, two megafires ignited in northern Colorado. The first, in August, was the Cameron Peak Fire north of Rocky Mountain National Park, which extended well into the remote northern reaches of the park. Then, in mid-October, when we are used to thinking fire season is over, the East Troublesome Creek Fire started and absolutely blew up, traveling tens of miles per day heading east, burning around the town of Grand Lake, and east into the park. High winds carrying firebrands thousands of feet ahead of the burning front account for abnormal rate of spread. In less than one day, the fire grew an unheard-of more than 120,000 acres, or 187 square miles.

Recall the fire regime concept. These fires were in lodgepole and spruce-fir forests and were mostly of high severity. These types of fires burn on a several-centuries fire return interval and are stand replacing (high severity).

The ferocious fire burned uphill on the west side of the park and actually jumped the alpine terrain along the Continental Divide and then burned down into the eastern side of the park, forcing evacuation of the town of Estes Park and creating months-long clouds of smoke over the Front Range communities.

Despite all efforts to control these fires, Grand Lake proper, the Colorado State University Pingree Park campus, and Estes Park were saved only by the vagaries of weather and heroic efforts by men and women working the fire lines and dropping retardant. Many outlying homes and cabins were destroyed by both fires. Both fires were only extinguished by winter snows in early December. Two years ago, scientists were saying that nationwide, our fire season is already two months longer than it used to be. Now many are saying the fire season is year-round, especially at low elevations. Besides destroying homes and buildings, wildfire is transforming wildlife habitat in Colorado.

The year before the fire, Anne and I did a three-day backpack loop in Rocky Mountain National Park starting near Bear Lake on the east of the Divide, hiking over Flattop Mountain to the Divide and westerly down into Grand Lake. Most of this entire area is now burned over from the East Troublesome Creek Fire, the second largest in state history. This fire burned nearly 200,000 acres, of which 30,000 acres were in the park (National Interagency Fire Center n.d.).

On Day 2 we hiked into Big Meadows and Upper Tonahutu Creek. This trail is prime moose and other wildlife habitat; we saw bull moose and bull elk sparring during the fall rut, right near our tent! The ruckus went on through all hours of the night, and we slept (tried to sleep) with our bear spray handy in case the brawling spilled over into our campsite. But it was a rare wilderness experience, and we savored it. The next day, we continued our loop hike back to the Divide.

By the turn of the twentieth century, elk herds were decimated by market hunters. In 1916, Colorado imported fifty elk from Wyoming to reestablish dwindling herds. The elk were transported and released in Idaho Springs and the Greenhorn Mountains in Pueblo County. From these limited transplants, and through decades of trapping and relocation efforts by wildlife managers, elk populations have soared to the abundant herds for which Colorado is now famous. Elk were more common to see along the CT when I hiked it twenty years ago. Today, with more hikers, elk are shyer and stay out of sight of the trail during daylight hours. Early mornings are a good time to see them, especially on the tundra, where they graze the nutritious alpine grasses and forbs.

At over 280,000 animals, Colorado's elk population is the largest in the world. Through hunting and wildlife viewing, elk bring visitors from many countries. In the fall people come to see these magnificent animals and to hear their distinctive bugle. In the fall, elk also lure hunters deep into the woods in a time-honored tradition and a critical management tool to thin the population. I have to say that I oppose trophy hunting. It eliminates the largest and strongest males; it prevents them from reproducing and in time weakens the gene pool. Predators, on the other hand, tend to take the weakest prey, leaving the strongest to reproduce. According to Colorado Parks and Wildlife (2023b), though, hunting is the most effective method to provide for herd health and critical funding to support conservation and research that benefits all of Colorado's wild spaces.

The agency is almost completely funded from hunting and fishing licenses (especially nonresident hunters), so of course they are proud of these burgeoning populations. The species not only provides aesthetic and sporting values for Coloradans but is also extremely important to local and state economies from licenses, outfitters, vehicles, gasoline, rifles, ammunition, motels, and restaurants.

In Rocky Mountain National Park, elk have significantly overgrazed the available range and rangers have resorted to fencing riparian areas and hiring professional hunters to cull (kill) surplus elk. The recent burn areas should stimulate more forage for elk, and numbers will grow. Elk killing hasn't been adequate to the need and perhaps wolves will do the culling for free when they are introduced in the state later in 2023. Wolves are not scheduled to be introduced into the park but are likely to arrive on their own.

I am thankful we got to see this area of the park before it was reduced to char and ruins, but I am sad it won't be the same for decades, if ever. Much of the park portions are rated moderate fire soil severity, and reforestation will likely be slow, at best. Prospects are better for aspen, which often resprout from roots. Lodgepole pine have serotinous cones that fires help open and enable to germinate. If previously beetle killed, lodgepole regeneration may be sparse. The fire-adapted lodgepole will hopefully be back in decades, but the higher-elevation spruce-fir forest is less resilient from wildfire and may take a century or, because of warming, may never return except near seed trees or moist areas.

I returned to this area in 2023 to see the extent of recovery. After a wet winter and spring, the understory in most places was lush even with no tree canopy. It was a stark view of green and looming black and tan burned tree trunks. It was disappointing not to see any conifer regeneration, but the thick understory may be hiding tender new seedlings. Moose appear to be thriving in burned areas, as one crossed our path and other hikers reported seeing other moose. In another hike behind the Kawaneeche Visitor Center, I did see thousands of lodgepole seedlings.

These two fires are the largest in state history and burned a mind-boggling 629 square miles. Together with other big fires in recent decades, this amount of wildfire is unsustainable for healthy forests. Many small fires are good for the forest and landscape to reduce fuel loads and create new habitat; megafires have such high intensity that they sterilize the soil and plant roots, are subject to massive erosion and mudslides, and do not reforest well, if at all.

A year later, on December 30, 2021, the catastrophic Marshall grass fire nearly consumed the towns of Superior and Louisville, Colorado, a late fire season date unprecedented in state history. This fire behavior was caused by extended drought, extremely dry fine fuels, lack of snow, and 100 mph hurricane winds that pushed the fire 5 mi. in only one hour. Thirty thousand people were evacuated. Over 1,100 homes and commercial buildings were destroyed, making it the most destructive fire in terms of property loss in Colorado history. As of this writing, two people died in the blaze. The National Oceanic and Atmospheric Administrative (NOAA) pronounced those six months as the warmest in state and national history. Like COVID-19, climate change is among us. Do we not yet have enough evidence to act?

A few months later, the Boulder NCAR wildfire burned several hundred acres in one of the premier urban hiking parks in Colorado and immediately adjacent to Boulder. It burned grassland and pine forest below the famous "flatirons," huge, scenic rock outcrops shaped like irons at a 45° angle. The fire came within a few hundred yards of over 1,000 upscale Boulder homes in the Table Mountain neighborhoods—the wildland-urban interface (WUI). Boulder park officials are taking credit for the thinning projects that have been underway for many years. It is too early to know if thinning or snowfall helped to contain the fire.

I feel the loss personally as I have hiked these trails over a hundred times; the place has an iconic beauty unmatched in the state. The nearby homes have ponderosa pine forests as well as landscaping that would have stoked the fire, and it could have been another tragedy for Boulder County. In fact, there have now been five wildfires with significant property damage and forest loss in Boulder County in the last twelve years.

The extraordinary Colorado wildfire seasons since 1996 have lasting effects on the landscape, both in the immediate area and locations that may be several miles away. Locations downhill and downstream from burned areas are very susceptible to flash flooding and debris flows, especially near steep terrain. Without vegetation, rainfall that would normally infiltrate the soil will run off extremely quickly after a wildfire, as the burned soil can be as water repellent as pavement. Massive quantities of topsoil centuries in the making are lost.

"Forest health" is defined by the Forest Service (n.d.b) as "production of forest conditions which directly satisfy human needs and by resilience, recurrence, persistence, and biophysical processes which lead to sustainable ecological conditions." Interesting that it is first defined in terms of satisfying human needs and second in terms of sustainable ecological conditions, as the two are often in conflict. Can we even have human needs without sustainable ecosystems?

Threats to Ecosystem Services

Ecosystem services are commonly defined as benefits people obtain from ecosystems. The Millennium Ecosystem Assessment (Millennium Ecosystem Reports n.d.)—a four-year United Nations assessment of the condition and trends of the world's ecosystems—categorizes ecosystem services as the provision of food, fresh water, fuel, fiber, and other goods; regulation services such as climate, water, and disease regulation, as well as pollination; supporting services such as soil formation and nutrient cycling; and cultural services such as educational, aesthetic, and cultural heritage values, as well as recreation and tourism. Colorado's outdoor recreation economy generates $62.5 billion in consumer spending annually and contributes 511,000 direct jobs according to state government sources; more modest estimates are available from the Outdoor Industry Association. Differences are due to what's included, such as more urban recreation.

Our public lands and forests provide these natural services that we don't even pay for and are worth trillions. In particular, mountain environments along the CT modify our climate, accumulate and store immense snowpack, and dispense mostly predictable, precious stream flows to our towns, cities, and farms in Colorado and throughout the Southwest.

Water managers and scientists attempt to measure and forecast river basin runoff each year. According to Western Water Assessment (Lukas 2014; Woelders 2020), in Colorado, 50–70 percent of the annual runoff is from melting snowpack. Not all of the snowpack reaches streams; 10–20 percent is lost from sublimation (direct evaporation from snow) and evaporation. A fraction recharges groundwater, wets soil, and is taken up by the forest. Forest water uptake is subsequently lost to transpiration.

Our recent 2023 high snowpack levels do not necessarily mean high runoff. If soil moisture levels are low, the soil acts as a sponge, absorbing more snowmelt, as was the case in the South Platte Basin in 2019–2020. Last year, though, the summer monsoon brought soil moisture levels up, and 2022 runoff should parallel snowpack. Hydrologists use sophisticated models to predict runoff, and soil moisture is an important variable. The winter snows of 2022–2023 were greatly above average and have brought us out of our twenty-year drought for the time being.

With climate change, the trend of decreased snowpack water reflects multiple effects of the projected warming: a shift toward precipitation falling as rain instead of snow, greater sublimation and melt of the snowpack throughout the season, and a shift toward earlier snowmelt in the spring. The general midrange of the projected change in snow water by midcentury is a loss of roughly 10 to 20 percent. This change is on top of a decline over the last thirty years. This may be too conservative an estimate. Elsewhere, I present more recent work that the snowpack may completely disappear by midcentury. Climate change is upsetting the water cycle in our state with consequences we all will regret.

In the Southern Rocky Mountains, desert dust deposition on mountain snowpack in winter, a consequence of land use disturbance in nearby arid regions, also leads to more rapid snowmelt. The effects of dust on snow have far-reaching human implications related to water resources.

While our forests require water resources, they produce oxygen for us to breathe and have historically sequestered carbon dioxide into carbon (wood). However, studies are showing those huge conflagrations—like the 2020 fires combined with severe bark beetle infestations and disease outbreaks—have left large swaths of dead, decomposing trees in most of our forests. Research by Grant Domke and others (2020) shows those dead trees are releasing massive amounts of carbon dioxide, turning the region into a net emitter of carbon dioxide rather than a carbon dioxide sponge. The reversal, which has already occurred in Colorado and is anticipated in several other states, is the result of misguided forest management practices and a changing climate, forest experts say.

Another ecological consequence of megafires is mud and runoff. Vegetation intercepts the precipitation, and the roots hold the soil together. High-severity fires make soils hydrophobic, and the result is nearly 100 percent runoff and soil erosion. Flash flooding results in streams carrying huge amounts of sediment. In 1996, the Buffalo Creek Fire and subsequent heavy rains in 1997 and 1998 led to very damaging mudslides. The storm waters deposited thousands of tons of coarse sediment and debris into Strontia Springs Reservoir downstream of Buffalo and Spring Creeks on the South Platte River. Approximately fifteen years' worth of sediments were deposited in the lake, reducing the reservoir's storage capacity by a third. We depend on our higher-elevation watersheds for water supply, and these structures can be heavily damaged and water supply interrupted. In addition, riparian and fishery habitat along streams and rivers can be destroyed for miles.

In 2021, mudslides and debris flows from the Grizzly Creek Fire of 2020 washed over I-70 in Glenwood Canyon, closing the major east-west artery through Colorado for a month and dumping 100,000 cu. yd. of soil and sediment into the Colorado River. The Cache la Poudre River ran black with ash for months from the Cameron Peak Fire, upsetting water supplies for northern Colorado. Nearly all Colorado cities and towns depend on mountain watersheds, and some have had to close water intakes for weeks to months in 2021 and exceed budgets for water treatment.

Recent modeling work by Danielle Touma and others (2022) project that more than 90 percent of extreme fire weather events in California, Colorado, and the Pacific Northwest will be followed by at least three extreme rainfall events within five years. Our results point to a future with substantially increased postfire hydrologic risks across much of the western United States.

Most scientists believe the warming and drying conditions in the last decade and, especially, last year, are a harbinger of even worse insect mortality and wildfire conditions in the future as our climate changes due to greenhouse gases. Our ability to preserve our forests will come down to our ability to reduce greenhouse gases in the atmosphere and, indeed, to change our way of life. Americans have thrived on fossil fuels, creating urban sprawl and a wasteful way of life that we equate to "affluence." An average American "climate criminal's" carbon footprint is 15.5 tons/year of carbon dioxide equivalent. Only Australia and Saudi Arabia have higher ones. The United Kingdom's, by comparison, is 6. Americans must go on a strict carbon diet.

In the new normal, the politics of climate change mirror the politics of the pandemic. The same people who oppose vaccinations and masking oppose any climate change solutions. Katharine Hayhoe, in her book *Saving Us*, explains that "[the] resistance to climate change is really a rejection of what people perceive to be unpleasant or unpalatable solutions [and] is known as *solution aversion*. And further, anything that threatens their tribal identity and ideology is something to be denied and it is based on fear of change and government control" (2021, 134). Because saying "it's not real" is our defense mechanism. Others argue human decision-making on complex issues to be guided not so much by reason but the tribal in-group/out-group affiliations. If scientists are not in your in-group, you tend to discount them or even assign evil intentions.

Misinformation and disinformation worked for many years for tobacco companies, who used media advertisements to fight scientists' claims that tobacco harms human health. Some political action groups funded by the fossil fuel industry are at work using the same model that the dangers of climate change are exaggerated or even false. Increasingly, they use television or social media platforms used only by in-group conservatives.

It makes you wonder about the human brain's ability to comprehend the world today and whether we are evolved enough to move beyond primitive decision-making.

5

Our Public Lands

A Short History of Our Public Lands

Any story of the Colorado Trail and landscape conservation deserves some history of our public lands. I say "our" because of our unique history: they belong to you and me. A detailed history of our public lands is beyond my scope here, but there is a good summary by the Public Lands Foundation (2014). Through conquest and treaty settlements, lands were also obtained from Mexico, Canada, Russia, Spain, France, and England and Native Americans. All public lands were once "owned" by Native Americans, although their concept of ownership was territorial but communal and in harmony with the environment. European-American subjugation of Native Americans is a long and unjust story also beyond my scope except what I will say elsewhere about the Utes who lived in areas near the Colorado Trail.

To encourage settlement and development of the West, Congress passed laws during the 1800s authorizing the disposal of public lands to citizens, states, and private companies. The General Land Office, a predecessor of the present-day BLM, was established in 1812 within the Department of the

Treasury to oversee the survey and disposal of the public domain lands and to keep the federal land records.

Each new state that joined the Union gave up claim to federal public domain lands within its borders but received large acreages of public domain in land grants. These were to be leased or sold by the state to help raise funds for public schools, colleges, universities, and other public institutions in the state. State lands are the next-largest type of public lands, although many are not accessible. Over 40 million additional acres were transferred out of the public domain in railroad and wagon road land grants.

In 1860, Congress began passing a series of laws to facilitate the settlement and development of vast areas of public domain west of the Mississippi River by citizens and masses of immigrants moving to America for a better life. Among these laws were the Homestead Act (1862), Timber Culture Act (1873), Desert Land Act (1877), and Timber and Stone Act (1878). Congress passed the General Mining Law of 1872 to encourage exploration and development of the nation's mineral resources. Notably, the 1916 Stock-Raising Homestead Act encouraged sheep and cattle raising on public lands. Most of these laws required some level of development effort on the land before it could be purchased for prices ranging from $1.25 to $2.50 per acre, as set by statutes. An estimated 640 million acres, including both surface and mineral rights, were transferred to those who settled the Midwest and the West.

Today, most of our federal public lands are managed by the US Forest Service, BLM, or National Park Service (NPS). The National Forest System (US Forest Service n.d.c), managed by the US Forest Service, began with the Forest Reserve Act of 1891. It allowed the president to establish forest reserves from public domain lands to help conserve the forests and watersheds of the West and authorized the president to designate public lands in the West into what were then called "forest reserves." Responsibility for these reserves fell under the Department of the Interior until 1905, when President Theodore Roosevelt transferred their care to the Department of Agriculture's new US Forest Service. Gifford Pinchot led this new agency as its first chief, charged with caring for the newly renamed national forests. Over 160 million acres of the original public domain lands are in the National Forest System. Consequently, BLM inherited the lower-elevation arid lands the Forest Service did not want. The Colorado Trail traverses six national forests and also BLM public lands.

Congress established the Bureau of Land Management in 1946 by merging the US Grazing Service and the General Land Office. After the merger, BLM's field organization consisted of land offices located in the capitals of the twelve western states, and sixty district grazing offices scattered throughout the rural areas of the same states. The Bureau of Land Management's early years could be characterized as an era of clerks and cowboys, emphasizing Lands and Minerals operations. Ed Abbey once referred to BLM as the Bureau of Livestock and Mining.

The Bureau of Land Management did not get any real statutory authority until passage of the Federal Land Policy and Management Act of 1976. Having worked for many years for BLM, I have sympathy for the impossible job its managers have: to meet its multiple-use mission (grazing, logging, mining, and oil and gas drilling, to name a few) but to protect cultural, wildlife, and wilderness values at the same time. With conflicting missions to oversee, managers get squeezed by factions and sometimes don't make decisions in favor of land health. The Bureau of Land Management is our largest public land manager, although its lower-elevation lands are not extensive along the Colorado Trail. Washington politics don't help: they underfund the organization and play political football with BLM's Washington headquarters office.

The Bureau of Land Management and the Forest Service have a similar statutory multiple use mandate—to manage the lands for production of commodities as well as recreation and preservation. A mandate of multiple use of natural resources is synonymous with conservation, whereas protective designation of lands from human disturbance is called preservation. Often these management goals conflict, causing a tangled history of conflict and lawsuits that continue to occur today.

Wilderness in the Twenty-First Century

Most academics would agree that preservation means protection from human disturbance such as vehicles and roads, logging, mining, oil, gas drilling, and so forth. Conservation is more lenient and allows for multiple uses such as those just listed. Often land managers are forced to zone incompatible uses into different areas. Most land managers are compelled by law to manage for multiple use and consider their mission a conservation one in the sense that much of the land still supports native vegetation and wildlife, although often in an impaired way. Most of the disturbances listed cause soil erosion; noxious weeds; and noise, air, and water pollution that tend to impair the resource. When we speak of preservation, we normally think of wilderness, roadless areas, wildlife refuges, and various other administrative classifications that limit disturbance.

Our National Wilderness Preservation System (n.d.) protects federally managed wilderness areas designated for preservation in their natural condition. Wilderness areas are managed by four federal land management agencies: the National Park Service, the Forest Service, the US Fish and Wildlife Service, and BLM. According to the Wilderness Act of 1964, the term *wilderness* is defined as "an area where the earth and community of life are untrammeled by man, where man himself is a visitor who does not remain" and "an area of undeveloped Federal land retaining its primeval character and influence, without permanent improvements or human habitation, which is protected and managed so as to preserve its natural conditions." As of 2021, 803 wilderness areas have been designated, totaling 111,368,221 acres. The CT traverses six designated wilderness areas and one national monument.

The National Park Service is instructed by the National Park Service Organic Act of 1916 to have more of a preservation mandate than that of the Forest Service or BLM—specifically, to manage unimpaired the natural and cultural resources and values of the national park system for the enjoyment, education, and inspiration of this and future generations National Park Service (n.d.). The CT does not traverse any national parks, although its scenery rivals any national park. Climate change is not just affecting Colorado's mountain ecosystems. Michael Yochim writes authoritatively and pleadingly in his book *Requiem for America's Best Idea: National Parks in the Era of Climate Change* (2022) about similar climate effects in Olympic, Grand Canyon, Glacier, Yellowstone, and Yosemite National Parks.

While national parks struggle with the effects of climate change, they also have struggled with managing wildlife. Generally, no hunting, mining, logging, or development other than tourism or recreational facilities are permitted, although in the NPS's early years, predator control; poaching and feeding of elk, bears, and deer; and other wildlife "control" on national parks were very common. In some parks, elk overpopulated and damaged the range and were directly killed by NPS. Nonnative species such as burros have been killed or removed in national parks. In an interesting tragedy of the commons, without predators, nonnative wild horses and burros on BLM land have also overpopulated their BLM range, and, by statute, BLM is not permitted to kill them. Sterilization and adoption programs are ineffective, and an estimated 41,000 are kept in holding facilities.

In a seminal paper, Soule and Noss (1998) introduced the concept of *rewilding*. Rewilding means the restoration of large, connected wilderness areas that support wide-ranging keystone species such as apex predators. Wilderness and roadless areas are fairly well connected along the Continental Divide that the Colorado Trail traverses, especially from Camp Hale and the Holy Cross Wilderness, through the Weminuche and Hermosa, well over half of the CT. Preservationists are always fighting for more protections from human disturbance, be they wilderness or administrative protections like the Hermosa. These areas offer opportunities for rewilding; already lynx and moose have been reintroduced in this area, wolves may eventually migrate into this area, and there has been talk at Colorado Parks and Wildlife about reintroducing wolverines. Although scientists believe large carnivores help ecosystem health and biodiversity, what will climate change do? Although not disturbance in a physical sense, warming and drying of the landscape will favor certain species and threaten others. This is a question I will return to later in chapter 6.

Our public lands are a legacy and a treasure left to us, the people, like no other in the world. We must care for them and protect them from overuse and abuse. Often, agencies charged with managing them are underfunded, understaffed, and subject to powerful political interests that want to develop water, cheaply graze livestock, cheaply extract the public's minerals, log the forests, and many other monetizing uses too numerous to mention. Sagebrush Rebels argue our public lands are illegal based on their interpretation of the Constitution, but legal scholars disagree.

Hikers can't solve these intractable problems, but how can we minimize our impact on the trail? As I wrote about in *Triple Crown Hiking Adventures*, even our most pristine wilderness areas are subject to man's influence through overcrowding, air pollution, and climate change. I teach wilderness skills for the Colorado Mountain Club, including Leave No Trace (n.d.). I teach and practice LNT principles. We plan ahead and prepare, we don't leave any litter at all and even pick up litter from others, we camp on durable surfaces so as not to impact vegetation, we don't make campfires, we bury human waste in 6" catholes 200' from any water or carry it out in Wag Bags, we don't use soap in streams, we respect wildlife, and we are considerate of others. The CT draws hikers from around the world. To fight climate change, we need to think about what hikers can do to reduce their carbon footprint. One way is by purchasing carbon offsets from reputable organizations. It is also foreseeable that a permit system will be instituted to alleviate hiker crowding. Backpacking permits are already common in national parks and certain national forests and long trails.

It's a start but not enough by itself. Land managers are already stepping up issuance of camping permits, timed entry permits, parking fees, closure areas, and other tools to control use. It is another form of the new normal. With the crush of population growth, public lands are under growing pressure to produce more energy, more cows, more wood products, more roads, and more recreation amenities. Constant vigilance by preservationists will be needed to protect what we have.

FIGURE 1. Grasshopper, Speed (me), Frosty at Monarch Pass trailhead.

FIGURE 2. Grasshopper taking a shower in an icy waterfall (no soap).

FIGURE 3. Bull moose near camp in La Garita Wilderness.

FIGURE 4. High mountain traverse so common along the Colorado Trail.

FIGURE 5. Speed at Colorado Trail sign.

FIGURE 6. Dead subalpine spruce forest. We hiked through almost 100 mi. of dead and dying forest.

FIGURE 7. Dead subalpine spruce forest at sunrise. We traversed nearly 100 mi. of dead or dying forest.

FIGURE 8. Healthy subalpine Engelmann spruce forest west of Highway 550. Spruce beetles have not arrived in this area.

FIGURE 9. Gudy's Rest overlooking Junction Creek near Durango trailhead.

FIGURE 10. Speed (me) at trail's end in Durango.

6

Monarch Pass to Creede

Subalpine and Alpine

In the Land of Ouray

In the year 2021, Colorado was again in extreme drought situation, especially on the Western Slope of the Continental Divide. The pandemic was continuing, with hundreds of thousands of dead in the US.

This year's hike was almost entirely on the Western Slope, so we were hoping for a wildfire- and smoke-free hike and adequate water sources. I kept a journal for this year's 2021 hike and made a report for each day. This section of the trail begins on the Monarch Crest at subalpine forest for many miles before gradually descending into upper montane forest along the Cochetopa Drainage, then begins to climb again into the alpine to nearby San Luis Peak, over 14,000'.

I was joined by friends Frosty and Grasshopper, who had not met in person yet. We three had been planning and anticipating this hike all winter and spring. Frosty is about my age and in good shape. We met in Colorado Mountain Club hikes up Pikes Peak in the winter and summer backpacks. Frosty had not done as much backpacking as Grasshopper and I and had worked to reduce his pack weight for this trip from over 30 lb. to around 20 lb. (not including food). He acquired a new tent, sleeping bag, and pad, along with trimming other items.

Frosty's trail name comes from his white beard. Frosty is a good ol' boy from Texas and grew up on a farm but went on to work in the oil business. Frosty likes his old country music and will belt out Jerry Jeff Walker and others with the slightest provocation. Grasshopper grew up in Texas, and the two men immediately bonded over music. Like us, Frosty is a grandfather who dotes on his grandchildren. Just the nicest two guys to hike with. Frosty is a tireless advocate for the Colorado Mountain Club, where he welcomes new members, and the Colorado Trail Foundation, where he has performed many days of trail maintenance.

We were all fully vaccinated and became comfortable together. The night before we started, we had a nice dinner in Salida with Frosty's wife, Kathy. Salida is one of the great trail towns on the CT. It is a bit of a hitch from near Monarch Pass but has great motels and restaurants, a hot springs pool, and resupply stores. Most of the motels are on Highway 50 on the southwest side from downtown, but downtown has better restaurants and is worth visiting. Salida is nestled at the eastern edge of the Arkansas Valley. The picturesque Arkansas River flows through town. When the Denver and Rio Grande Western Railroad arrived in 1880, Salida became the seat of Chaffee County, which was formed in 1879. The railroad set up a townsite, and the summer of 1880 brought a building frenzy to the once-peaceful valley. Buildings could not be put up fast enough for the arriving townspeople and miners. Gold had been first discovered in Chaffee County back in 1859 in the creeks along the Arkansas River. Placer mining commenced, and within the first ten years around $400,000 of gold had been mined from the area.

Of interest to me, maybe Salida's greatest contribution to the mining of gold, silver, lead, and zinc in central Colorado was its smelters. When ore is extracted from the earth, it is locked in the hard rock that surrounds it. Through a series of applications of heat and chemicals, the precious metal was extracted. By 1909, Salida boasted six smelting furnaces and twelve roasters. The plant could process up to 1,500 tons of ore a day and employed up to 500 people at one time. In 1917, a 365' tall smokestack was added to the smelter plant north of town to help disperse the dangerous chemicals that are a by-product of smelting. Previously, smaller smokestacks were in place, allowing the noxious fumes to travel down into Arkansas Valley, where it poisoned farmland and animals. In my career, I worked on several smelter sites in Idaho and Montana, assessing large-scale soil contamination problems. Today, only the old stack remains.

We three camped at Monarch Spur RV Park and Campground along the South Arkansas River, really a medium-sized creek. There was a flash flood warning at the time, and it was raining with some distant thunder. At least we got tents up before rain. We were hoping for a safe evening. Highway 50 truck traffic nearby was noisy. Frosty and I sat in the car in the dark and rain for a while chatting about the world's problems. It rained four hours with lots of boomers.

We planned a moderate itinerary, averaging about 12–15 mi. a day early on. The idea is to start out with lower-mileage days to acclimatize and build leg strength and avoid overuse injuries. Although I am comfortable with 20+ mi. days, we agreed to start out doing fewer miles and work our way into 15 mi. days in a week or so.

In the morning, we left a car at Monarch Pass and hiked out early. Our packs were loaded with seven days of food and wet tents. With these 9 lb. of food and a liter of water, my pack was about 23 lb. I am an ultralight hiker. I often teach others how to lighten their heavy packs. I can recall carrying 50 lb. in my external-framed Kelty pack back in the 1970s. That pack weighed 6 lb. empty! Today I carry a 30° 19 oz. sleeping bag, a 1 lb. tent, a 12 oz. inflatable pad, a small stove, an Ursack for hanging my food bag, a lightweight fleece and down vest, and various small first-aid and hygiene essential items. That's about it. I wear trail runners that are not waterproof and dry quickly after fords or rainstorms. They are much lighter than the old leather boots I used to wear, and I rarely get blisters. I have used trekking poles ever since my first long hike on the John Muir Trail, courtesy of Grasshopper's teachings. I have found that with this light pack, I can hike 20–30 mi. per day even while in my sixties. I enjoy the hike much more because I am not as easily fatigued nor have any shoulder or back pain.

In wilderness classes I teach, I am often asked about the food I take. Of course, it's a very individual decision. I am not too choosy on the trail as long as the food is calorie dense, meaning packing an average of 150 cal per oz. Breakfast for me is granola, oatmeal, or a Pop-Tart. I have a midmorning snack of a bar or dried fruit, followed by a big lunch. My lunch usually has peanut butter and crackers, maybe some cheese, dried fruit, and chips. Peanut butter and chips pack about 180 cal per oz., and the chips provide much-needed electrolytes. I have an afternoon snack like a bar, and my dinner is usually a freeze-dried one, possibly with some cookies for dessert. My food averages about 3,000 cal or 1.25 lb. per day, so my seven-day food bag weighed about 10 lb.

Backpackers in high altitudes burn over 200–300 cal per hour. I often hike 10–12 hours per day, so, in addition to basal metabolism (as if you sat around all day), I burn 4,000–6,000 cal per day. It is difficult to carry this much food, so I make up for the deficit by binge-eating in town stops every 5–7 days when I resupply. I often mail a food box to myself via general delivery or shop in a local grocery.

In the first 8 mi. on the Monarch Crest over 11,000', we experienced over 100 bicycles all morning riding from behind and several dirt bikes. Most of the riders were courteous but impatient to pass. Several riders cut a trail curve riding over vegetation to pass. I don't mind stepping aside, but I don't like to trample trailside vegetation, so I would look for a good place to pull over. Some bikers repeated their request to pass, and I tossed words over my shoulder to "hold on a second." It is still a bit of shock during a quiet hike to dodge noisy, fast-moving riders who almost always are in a pack. There is some evidence that wildlife are more impacted by bikes than by hikers. My partners were more tolerant than I was. This wasn't the wilderness experience I had envisioned.

In just a few miles from Marshall Pass, we passed very near Mount Ouray, 13,971', and nearby Mount Chipeta, 13,472'. Born in 1883, Ouray was a chief of the Tabeguache (Uncompahgre) band of the Ute Tribe, located in western Colorado. Chipeta was his wife. He became a chief when the Utes claimed all of the Colorado mountains. Because of his leadership abilities, Ouray was acknowledged by the US government as a chief of the Utes and he traveled to Washington, DC, to negotiate for the welfare of the Utes. Raised in the culturally diverse town of Taos, Ouray learned to speak many languages, which helped him in the negotiations with the whites. He carried a burden of grief over his five-year-old son, who was abducted during an attack by the Sioux. Soon after the Civil War, some Ute leaders, including Chief Ouray, agreed to the Treaty of 1868. This founded a reservation that covered nearly all of Colorado west of the Continental Divide.

I am attracted to Ouray because in some ways, he reminds me of my father. Not that I ever knew Ouray of course; what I know are mostly white historians' views of him. Ouray was more of a negotiator than my dad. Ouray was a charismatic leader with great integrity, as was my dad. Like Ouray, my dad was physically imposing, and others looked to him for leadership. People idolized my dad because he was an FBI agent, something of a novelty in those days. Besides that, he had Lakota Sioux ancestry and made or had made several authentic costumes, replete with eagle feather headdress and bustle. He made a full-size tipi and tanned a cowhide for Indian drums. He took every opportunity to show off the costume and educate us all about Indians.

A story of his eagle feathers is worth mentioning. When we lived in Wyoming near the Wind River Indian Reservation, the local fish and game officer found some dead golden eagles, apparently electrocuted on a powerline and, knowing my Dad was part Indian and in federal law enforcement, brought him the carcasses. It is illegal for people other than Indians to possess eagle parts, so Dad called the federal magistrate, who told him he could have them since he was on the rolls of the tribe in South Dakota. Instead, Dad donated them to Arapaho friends on the reservation, who seemed glad to have them. Months later, to his surprise, they returned with a beautiful eagle headdress and bustle they had crafted as gifts to him. Dad initially refused them, but the federal magistrate said to take them. In a way, I think he kept them to help educate people about Indians. When Dad passed, I initially loaned the eagle items and tipi to the Koshare Kiva (a boy-scout-renowned American Indian museum in La Junta). A couple of years later, I found out they were just in storage, so I reclaimed them and donated them to some Cheyenne and Lakota dancers who were performing locally. So, they were repatriated to Native Americans after nearly fifty years. I kept the rest of his costume.

My dad was the first in his family to graduate from college. He did not study science but, rather, chose fine arts. He introduced my brother and me and the neighborhood kids to Scouting, and despite its recent bad press Scouting was a major, positive force in my childhood and for my friends too. Dad devoted over a decade of his life to Scouting, always being the main adult leader. He was a constant for us and took us all camping and backpacking. He provided the access to nature for me that I will never forget. I hope I repaid it to my children. As a family we traveled to Colorado every year, where I fell in love with the mountains, forests, and streams—places Ouray loved also.

Ouray was a man of keen perceptions and a talented diplomat, a negotiator, and a peacekeeper; many believe Ouray was the greatest of all chiefs (Athearn 1977; Smith 1986). He met with Presidents Abraham Lincoln, Ulysses S. Grant, and Rutherford B. Hayes and was called the man of peace because he sought to make treaties with settlers and the government. Ouray traveled Colorado by foot and wagon and by the early railroads in several visits to Washington, DC. Imagine his impressions of the train, the armies, and the cities he visited even though he was himself somewhat worldly for an Indian. He saw Colorado become a state in 1876. Following the Meeker Massacre (White River War) of 1879, he traveled in 1880 to Washington, DC. He tried to secure a treaty for the Uncompahgre Utes, who wanted to stay in Colorado; but, the following year, the United States forced the Uncompahgre and the White River Utes to reservations in present-day Utah. It was the end of a long, bitter struggle for the Mountain Utes, and Ouray died shortly after in 1880. His wife, Chipeta, was also highly respected by the Utes and whites and lived another forty-four years. After Ouray's death, miners and railroads had poured into Leadville, Salida, Creede, Lake City, and Silverton and were transforming the landscape. Like the bison, his people were all but gone from the state. Probably he was heartbroken. He had a farm near Montrose on the Uncompahgre River at the Second Los Piños Agency. He is buried in the cemetery in Ignacio.

Being part Native American, I often wonder what it was like to have your land and home stripped from you by invaders who slaughter you with disease and guns, don't honor their own treaties, and ship survivors away like cattle. I can't help comparing Ouray with Martin Luther King Jr. Both were charismatic leaders of color who suffered hate with grace and preached nonviolence. Ouray was not assassinated but was in constant threat of his life. Both died at a time of greatest despair for their people. Whereas Black Americans gained the vote in 1870, it took another forty-four years for Indians to gain that right. Thinking of the history of this land makes for a somber but richer hike. The scope of change on the landscape and on lifestyles that has occurred in the century and a half since Ouray's time is simply breathtaking. Our lives and the landscape today would strain his imagination and mostly not in a good way.

Colorado's population in Ouray's time was estimated to be around 30,000–50,000 (figure from 1870 Historical Census: Demographic Statistics

2023); Utes numbered only a few thousand. Our population was about 1.3 million when I was born and currently is just shy of 6 million (State of Colorado n.d.), growing nearly fivefold in my lifetime. Prior to the pandemic, Colorado had the second-fastest growth rate of any state in the country, at 1.85 percent, which doubles every thirty-seven years. At this rate, my children could see 12 million in the state, and I shudder to think about my grandchildren. Ouray would be appalled at a 50 mi. wide megalopolis stretching from Cheyenne to Trinidad and every mountain valley filled with development. (The growth rate has slowed since the pandemic and hopefully will eventually stabilize near zero.) That kind of growth rate is unsustainable from airshed, climate, and watershed standpoints, and our forests, wildlife, and ski areas may disappear. Our public lands, if they indeed survive, will be even more degraded by grazing, overcrowding, motorized vehicles, oil and gas, logging, and mining. Coloradans will have to put the brakes on growth if we want to preserve the qualities we have enjoyed in our state. Ouray and his people lived in a time of a small, stable population that, aside from occasionally burning the forest to make it more productive, was in harmony with the environment.

Grasshopper had climbed Mount Ouray from the CT on a previous hike. It's a steep 2,300' climb from the trail, but we elected to pass it by today. I would like to go back to pay my symbolic respects to Ouray.

It drizzled and rained most of the day, and I broke out all my rain gear. We camped in nice area at Marshall Pass, at 10,842'. In 1881, the narrow-gauge mainline of the Denver and Rio Grande Western Railroad was built across Marshall Pass on the way from Denver to Salt Lake City. This railroad line was completed before the Denver, South Park and Pacific Railroad completed the Alpine Tunnel, so it was the first crossing of the Continental Divide in Colorado by any railroad. The railroad was closed in 1955, and the tracks are gone. As there is a forest road, parking lot, and privy here, there were motorbikes too. We got to camp in the early afternoon, did camp chores, and dried the tents.

I took a short walk around, meeting a trio of young women hikers who tented nearby. Because of our timing of midsummer, there were almost no mosquitoes. The dirt bikes were annoying until 7 p.m. They are allowed in a few areas, but we saw them in unauthorized areas too. I closed up my tent that night during a rainstorm, and my sleeping bag got a little wet at the foot from condensation off the tent walls. My legs were tired, but my pack weight filled with food was fine.

It cleared, and we enjoyed a full moon that night. The next morning, we were out about 7 a.m.; it was mostly clear and cool in the fifties. We had stiff climbing as we ascended the 11,885' Windy Peak and were passed by half dozen hikers. Descending, we saw many beautiful flowers on this day, especially at about mile 271. Colorado columbines (Colorado's state flower), tall larkspurs, chiming bells, paintbrushes, arnicas, senecios, showy daisies, ram's horns. The wildflower bloom was terrific in 2021, despite very low winter snowpack. Heavy monsoon rains saved the day for flowers this year and many seeds will be available for the next few years, but prolonged drought years can affect reproduction.

Running between the San Juan Mountains and Sawatch Range is a 16 mi. length of the Continental Divide connected by lower-elevation mountains, mostly dry pine forest, and grasslands. Overlooked so far for designated wilderness, the Cochetopa Hills contain wilderness values as a wildlife and native plant corridor between the ranges. The Ute word *Cochetopa* means "Pass of the Buffalo"; of course, the buffalo are long gone, replaced by cattle in the valleys. The historic range of bison in Colorado is not well known, but the nearby San Luis Valley is well documented to have had bison, and it is likely they moved over Cochetopa Pass into the Cochetopa and Gunnison Valleys and were hunted by the Utes (Meaney and Van Duren 1993).

Interestingly, the last few bison in Colorado were poached and extirpated in Colorado in about 1897, in what is now the Lost Creek Wilderness. The poaching was widely reported, and the public outcry led to the first Department of Game, Fish and Forestry in the state. Bison Peak, 12,567', is the highest point in the wilderness but several miles from the CT. Although named for its rock formations, I wonder whether bison ever roamed those alpine areas.

We saw a few illegal dirt bikes this day. It rained after lunch for three hours, then the sun came out in time for camp. Grasshopper lost a trekking pole and spent several hours looking for it. We looked too. Fortunately, he doesn't use his poles for his tent. I bonked a mile before camp. Steady rain had prevented my snack, but a Snickers Bar at camp helped. Frosty and I were both tired, but Grasshopper was strong from hiking the week before on CT. We saw several bike packers near the end of our day. It rained for hours just after dinner. Squeezed between pole hunting and the rain, I'm not sure whether Grasshopper made a hot dinner. It was expected to clear the next day.

It rained for six hours that night, stopping finally at midnight. I had no leakage but plenty of condensation from having the tent closed up. I was a little cold in the night but forgot to check the temperature. We packed wet tents in the morning and left a little later than planned.

The trail led through some lovely high-altitude meadows on Sargents Mesa with a few cows. Frosty and I walked a quarter mile off trail to a water tank and the nearby Soldierstone Memorial. It is dedicated to soldiers lost in the Indochina wars, including Vietnam. It's a 10' engraved granite column with a miniature mortar on top surrounded by a parapet. There are plaques all around, a stone wall—all very professional. Why is it out here, miles from anywhere? (That depends on what you mean by "anywhere.") I think it must be the solace of the place? Dispersed about 50 yd. from the central marker are thirty-six heavy quote-stones etched in French, Laotian, Thai, Vietnamese, and Arabic, among other languages.

"The intent was to offer tribute from American soldiers to forgotten soldiers from 'Vietnam, Laos, Cambodia, the Hmong, the Montagnard Tribes of Central Vietnam, the Koreans, Thais, French, Germans, Slavs, North Africans, Black Africans and others of all religions and persuasions who willingly or unwillingly expended lives during the long wars lost in hopes, proud and vain, for the people of Indochina, 1945 through 1975'" (Hood n.d.).

Returning to the trail, we hiked through a long forest past Lake Baldy, where Grasshopper took a swim. It was a stiff hike down and back up to the lake, so Frosty and I passed on it and headed on to the next water source over two hills and another long meadow. Grasshopper caught up later, and we got water at the trickle of Razor Creek.

We camped near the trail along the nearly-dry creek. I was near the creek and hoped to avoid condensation or cold. A kid named Rocky appears to have joined us. It rained hard immediately after dinner, and we scattered to the tents.

An unsupported CT bike race from Durango to Denver was happening, and the leaders passed me riding in the middle of the night. With no more rain during the night, I slept a little better that night. We were out about 7 a.m. We had interesting political discussions about all the problems of overcrowding of our recreation areas, overpopulation in a larger sense, and the degradation of our forests and entire planet. We talked about why we hike, the Zen-like nature fix it provides, brain chemistry, and the opportunity for solace from our problems.

Nature Fix

Have you ever wondered why you enjoy the out-of-doors no matter if you are a hiker, climber, paddler, backpacker, photographer, fisherman, hunter, or birder? Condensed into a single volume in an easily readable form, *The Nature Fix* by Florence Williams (2020) takes us around the world from Japan to Korea to Finland, Scotland, and other places in search of researchers who are studying this very question.

Psychologists, neurobiologists, physicians, and others are increasingly using science to identify biomarkers of our happiness and of our stress. Noise and air pollution, work stress, tech devices, video gaming—all these things disconnect us from the outdoors and natural healing. Researchers are finding that at least five hours per month is needed to alleviate stress and to provide balance to our hectic urban lives. Wild areas may be best, but even larger urban parks can offer relief. A dose-response curve even appears to be present; more is better. Other researchers advocate three hours per week to reduce depression, increase sociability, exercise, and self-esteem. Even forty minutes per day slows cognitive decline.

We experience the outdoors through all of our senses. Williams emphasizes the salubrious effect of pine scent, cypress oil aromatherapy, birdsong, the sound of water, even looking out windows and at paintings or photographs of the outdoors. In some countries, "forest bathing" is prescribed to those looking for that nature fix to slow their heart rate, reduce blood pressure, reduce stress-related cortisols, and increase natural killer T cells to help our immune response.

To put a finer point on the value of green spaces especially during the pandemic, University of Colorado Boulder researchers found significantly higher depression scores for all Covid periods compared to the "before Covid" period, and significantly higher anxiety scores during the "fall wave" of Covid compared to earlier periods (Reid, Rieves, and Carlson 2022). Adjusted for sociodemographic and pandemic stressors, they found that spending a lot of time in green space was associated significantly with lower anxiety and depression. They also observed significantly lower depression scores associated with satellite data of green spaces and significantly lower anxiety scores with perceived abundance of green space. There was some evidence of lower anxiety scores for people reporting having high-quality green spaces near the home. This research provides further evidence of mental health benefits associated with green space exposure during the COVID-19 pandemic even after adjustment for sociodemographic variables and significant pandemic-related stressors. Sounds all very scientific, but it makes the point that people sought our trails and parks for solace during the pandemic.

As a hiker and naturalist, I always feel better during a hike when I can put aside the traffic, noise, tech devices; appreciate natural beauty; experience awe and quiet solitude. Or maybe it's my small slice of Lakota heritage that draws me to the green spaces. Whatever, with our burgeoning Colorado population, we need more wildlands to find solace in.

As John Muir so eloquently said, "Nature's peace will flow into you as sunshine flows into trees. The winds will blow their own freshness into you, and the storms their energy, while cares will drop off like autumn leaves" (Muir 1901, 59).

UFOs and Trail Magic

We have seen extensive beetle-kill forest mortality ever since Monarch, especially among spruce in the subalpine zone. Recent research by 2009 suggests that some drought- and beetle-resistant spruce are regenerating (Andrus, Hart, and Veblen 2020), but Tom Veblen (interview with author) believes we will see a shift toward subalpine fir and aspen in these areas as the climate warms. Spruce need cool, moist conditions to thrive as do aspen, but aspen tolerate warmer temperatures and resprout from roots in already-moist areas. We mounted a couple of big hills and then enjoyed a long descent in lodgepole pine toward North Pass, Highway 114.

We picked up Lujan Forest Road as it traversed beautiful aspen groves that gave me that forest bathing fix. We passed some logging operations and cows on BLM land. I have a bias against cattle especially on public lands. There is plenty of research showing the damage of overgrazing on public lands, especially historically in the late 1800s and first half of the 1900s, before BLM was formed and authority to regulate grazing was passed. Ken Reyher notes that even by 1890, it was clear that western Colorado range conditions had seriously declined. Grass between Delta and Grand Junction had been grazed almost out of existence. According to Ken Reyher (2002), the Utes used to burn these plateaus and mesas, but now pinyon and juniper have choked out the grass and dried up the streams. And, "it is a landscape that chief Ouray and those of his time would no longer recognize." Whether it was Ute burning or overgrazing, today that country is desert.

In spring in the nearby Gunnison area, the cows have their calves at home ranches in the valleys and begin moving up-valley or to higher rangelands. The home ranches where they have wintered can then begin the "huge process" of turning on irrigation and begin growing the tremendous amount of hay needed for the remaining year ahead. The lower elevation allows an earlier growing season, with its shallower snowpack, and the cows head to mid-altitude range, fresh with snowmelt across the meadows, for four of the Gunnison Valley's main ranches, all of which are family owned. After about a month at mid-elevation, ranchers move their cattle to yet higher altitudes. In September or October, ranchers return the cows either to market or the home ranch. Those mid-high elevation lands are typically public land grazing allotments administered by BLM or the Forest Service, for which ranchers pay a pittance in grazing fees.

Some western ranchers who are part of the antigovernment Sagebrush Rebellion don't pay their grazing fees. The Bundy family of Utah and Nevada are notorious for not paying millions of dollars of grazing fees for decades and showing up with armed militias when the government tried to impound their cattle. The same Bundys helped other ranchers orchestrate the takeover and occupation of the Malheur National Wildlife Refuge in Oregon that resulted in a shoot-out and significant damage to the Refuge (Wiles 2016). With these qualifications, Ammon Bundy ran for governor of Idaho. Fortunately, these ranchers are in a minority but are still a threat to our public lands.

In a recent interview by Colorado Public Radio (2021), nearby Gunnison Valley ranchers expressed great concern about climate change. Ranches that have been in the same family for over 100 years are struggling to feed their animals because the drought has dried up creeks and reduced the forage condition on their grazing allotments. They can't keep the cows on high-elevation summer allotments as long as they used to and have to bring them back earlier to the home ranch and feed the cows, which is expensive and upsets their balance sheets. They are experimenting with lower stocking rates on the range and rotational grazing using portable electric fencing. Several longtime ranches are predicting they will not be able to continue ranching if the megadrought continues.

Based on a lifetime of roaming the west and a career with BLM, depending on location, I think BLM does a poor-to-adequate job of regulating cattle on public lands. Ranchers get a subsidized lease on grazing allotments, many of which have been in the same family for generations. There is still damage to former grasslands that have converted to dry shrublands and pinyon-juniper woodlands, and damage to riparian areas. The Bureau of Land Management leases (large allotments) to ranchers, and the allotments are evaluated via BLM's own land-health standards. A large percentage of the allotments fail to meet BLM's own standards—because of livestock grazing (Bureau of Land Management n.d.). The Bureau of Land Management practices expensive mechanical chaining, mastication, poisoning, and cutting to remove pinyon, juniper, and sagebrush in an effort to restore grasses, but the real problem is overgrazing, including by wild horses. Stocking rates need to be terminated or reduced to allow recovery as the climate changes. An excellent case is made by Ketcham (2019) for removing cattle from public lands.

Consuming beef and milk is likely to become a luxury in the future as cattle raising's carbon footprint is extremely high. Livestock contributes 14.5 percent to worldwide greenhouse gas emissions according to the United Nations Food and Agriculture Organization (Gerber 2013). Cattle are responsible for the majority of emissions, as they belch methane in vast amounts from enteric fermentation. Methane is twenty-eight times more potent as a greenhouse gas than carbon dioxide. Cattle produce five to ten times more greenhouse gases than equivalent grams of protein from pork and chicken. So, consuming beef worsens climate change.

We had lunch at North Pass on Highway 113 near historic Cochetopa Pass. We then had several miles of sun-exposed hiking in sagebrush sprinkled with yellow balsamroot along Cochetopa Park. On the western slope of the Divide, sagebrush can replace the montane ecosystem at elevations up to 9,000'. We headed up the Pine Creek Valley back into the forest up a forgettable forest road. I don't remember this road from last time and wondered if the trail had been rerouted. Rocky, Frosty, and I found a nice flat space in the lodgepole forest to dry-camp; Grasshopper moved down the trail to camp.

We saw a dozen bike racers this day. We wondered where they are resupplied until we found out they are carrying everything for the entire trip to Denver. And they didn't have much gear aboard; I don't think they even sleep.

Resting in camp, I listened to music that takes me back to a simpler life in my youth. Like many long-distance hikers, I sometimes use earbuds to listen to my old rock and roll tunes. Similar to hiking, favorite songs cause a release of dopamine and serotonin in the brain and a sense of well-being.

Rocky left early and was going for big miles this day. Frosty and I met up with Grasshopper down the trail up on a hilltop. We heard Rocky found an iPhone near Grasshopper's camp. He sent it forward with a bike racer. Shortly after, we met a bike racer who had video of a UFO he had taken minutes ago. It looked like a flying saucer moving across the sky. Strange things happen on the trail.

We descended a long, exposed two-track road, crossing the dirt Cochetopa Pass, a flattish area that was used by the Utes and the bison, into enormous, sage-covered Cochetopa Park. The hike was through sunny meadows ringed by partially dead forest, thankfully still cool. We stopped for trail magic at a couple's RV camp nearby and had water and an apple and visited with trail angel Grasshopper and his wife. They took our trash too! They had all the glamping gear, including solar panels, a weather station, a charging station for hikers, and a hummingbird feeder.

We thanked them and headed out through more warm, exposed sagebrush meadows on a jeep road for five mi. until the road climbed into an aspen forest. In the late afternoon, we made camp in some aspens just off the trail.

Cochetopa Park is part of the crucial habitat for the federally threatened Gunnison sage-grouse. There are only about 5,000 of these birds left in the world. They require unfragmented sagebrush and associated wet meadows for their food supply. In some areas, cattle grazing and oil and gas development threaten their remaining habitat. Concern for the wet meadows drying up with climate change makes them very vulnerable. Unsurprisingly, we did not see any of these rare birds. They only flock together in April, when the males display white-breasted plumage and a spiky tail bustle. They strut and throw their shoulders forward as they dance for the females on leks, the locations of which are unique and known to the birds. They return to the same leks year after year. We did not see any sage grouse; they are very rare, after all.

I understand the Forest Service is working on a 32 mi. reroute in this section that would move the trail from the various roads to a single track. The current route is cow country. We walked through a herd of 100 Angus cattle. The water in the nearby creek was nasty, but we got water farther down the trail at Ant Creek. We had mostly easy jeep road walking this day, so we powered 16 mi. We carried water for a dry camp and some for the next morning in this 11 mi. waterless section.

We made camp in some stunted aspens near the trail. We met up with the trio of young women hikers we had met a few days ago on Marshall Pass. Frosty did his soft sell on the merits of joining the Colorado Mountain Club and Colorado Trail Foundation. They wanted to get some more miles in and hiked on.

Out at 7 a.m., and we hiked the cool frosty morning down to Cochetopa Creek. We had lovely views of the verdant valley and meandering stream and No Road! Hikers we passed said they had seen several moose that morning, but we missed them. The footbridge was washed out, so we forded the creek where it was about knee deep. I saw trout and nice pools and riffles. I love this stream! Just a few miles northwest of here is the site of the old Los Piños Agency, the location the Mountain Utes were to settle at under the Treaty of 1868. Although a pretty mountain valley, at over 9,000', it was without the vast traditional hunting grounds and the land was too cold and remote to farm. The agency was thus later transferred to the Uncompahgre River near Montrose (although it was still called the Los Piños Agency). Imagine Ouray's feelings for the white man who kept moving the Utes around like they were cattle. Speaking of cattle, today it is cattle country where the bison probably used to roam.

We encountered another ford just before we entered La Garita Wilderness, following Cochetopa Creek. It grew hot and exposed, but the Cochetopa Valley views were wonderful. There are a private ranch and some cattle, but it looked idyllic. Frosty was doing well. Grasshopper, of course too.

Biodiversity, Bison, Bees, and Butterflies

All is not charred forest and destruction. There are still some refuges for the wild things. Overlooked so far for designated wilderness, the Cochetopa Hills I was in contain wilderness values as a wildlife and native plant corridor between the ranges. As mentioned, the Ute word *Cochetopa* means Pass of the Buffalo; of course, the buffalo are long gone, replaced by cattle in the valleys.

It is also an area that contains great diversity and all the major forest types in Colorado including aspen, Douglas fir, white fir, subalpine fir, lodgepole pine, gnarled limber pine, ponderosa pine, Colorado blue spruce, and Engelmann spruce. Because of its modest scenery and remoteness, this area is lightly visited by hikers except Colorado Trail and CDT through-hikers and mountain bikers. Besides the typical elk and mule deer, the Cochetopa Hills have bighorn sheep and pronghorn antelope, unusual to find together. In June and early July, this area bursts with wildflowers along its riparian areas.

Bighorn sheep are an iconic species of the American West. They call some of our country's most rugged and remote landscapes home, ranging from the foothills to the alpine. Their cultural, ecological, aesthetic, and economic value has made bighorn sheep a vital part of North American heritage. Bighorns are the Colorado state mammal and the logo of Colorado Parks and Wildlife.

Bighorn sheep are extremely sensitive to changes in the environment and are considered an indicator species. Indicator species can signal changes in the biological health of an ecosystem, including climate change. Bighorn sheep exist in related populations, which means they move between mountain ranges to reproduce with other sheep populations in order to maintain genetic diversity. Thriving populations occur on interconnected landscapes, with corridors and contiguous swaths of habitat. So, a healthy, flourishing herd is indicative of a robust and flourishing ecosystem. Our herds are not that healthy, suffering from domestic sheep diseases and lack of genetic diversity. Climate corridors will be essential for their survival. Alas, we did not see bighorns on this trip, but I have seen them in various places in Colorado and elsewhere.

I get my nature fix from watching wildlife like bighorns, but part of my nature fix is observing and appreciating wildflowers and they are much easier to see. In many ways, wildflowers are symbolic of forest health, requiring adequate moisture at the right time, sunlight, and fertile soils. Some, like fireweed, are often the first colonizers after a wildfire. Like most angiosperms, wildflowers depend on pollinators for reproduction. Red, orange, and yellow flowers attract butterflies, while blue, purple, yellow, and white flowers appeal to bees. Colorado has many species of native bees and wasps that pollinate. A large number of fly species also pollinate. Hummingbirds favor the color red. Some flowers have colors in the ultraviolet spectrum that are invisible to humans but are highly attractive to bees.

The wondrous wildflowers are affected in different ways by the timing of snowmelt. Early snowmelt affects early-flowering species differently than late-flowering ones. For example, early snowmelt reduces soil moisture later in the season and therefore can have negative impacts on both early- and late-flowering species. Likewise, wildlife are affected by changes in snowmelt that alter habitat, food availability, competitors and predators, pests, the timing of hibernation, and other disturbances to the environment. Reductions in snowpack and increased temperatures have led to earlier breeding in amphibian species. Songbirds and other bird species may undergo changes in the timing of migration and breeding.

Most wildflowers rely on pollinators for reproduction. A pollinator can also detect a flower's scent and follows the concentration gradient of the chemical producing the scent to the flower. Plant species pollinated by bees and flies have sweet scents, and those pollinated by beetles have strong musty, spicy, or fruity odors. Flowers that use scents to attract their pollinators are generally drab in appearance, white or purple-brown to dark red-brown, and exude very strong scents that can be detected at a distance. Plants' scent levels tend to be highest when the flowers are ready for pollination and when potential pollinators are active. Bees or butterflies pollinate plants whose scent is high during the day, whereas moths and bats pollinate plants whose fragrance is greatest at night. Climate change is affecting pollinators, causing their life cycle to get out of sync with that of the wildflowers.

Our great biodiversity is a legacy of many eons of evolution and is closely attuned to climate. As climate changes, some species are lost or migrate, if they can. Wildflower and grass seeds that are wind-spread easily migrate, as do generalist animals like birds, elk, deer, black bears, coyotes, bobcats, and mountain lions, who are all mobile and adaptable. Moose, bighorn sheep, and lynx, not so much. Changing climate upsets the plant and animal community in ways that are structural as well as phenological. Phenology is the study of timing of plant bud break, flowering and pollination, bird migration, salmon migration, and so on. For example, if insect pollinators get out of timing with flowering, pollination fails.

For now, nature's intricacies never fail to give me a sense of wonder. For example, the diversity of flower shapes attracts certain pollinators and enables them to pick up and deliver pollen. Wide-open, radially symmetrical flowers such as buttercups and sunflowers allow easy access to many insects from beetles to butterflies, while bilaterally symmetrical flowers such as monkshoods appeal to bees who like to wiggle up inside enclosing petals. Some flowers like elephantellas use tricks such as trigger mechanisms that shoot pollen on an insect when it lands on specialized petals. Long tubular flowers such as scarlet gilias favor pollination by hummingbirds, whose long tongues are able to reach the nectar hidden deep inside.

The high-altitude wildflowers do not depend on the ubiquitous honeybee that pollinates most crops and ornamental trees, shrubs, and flowers. Colorado has over 946 native bee species but only 50 butterfly species. Native bees are indispensable to the health of the natural world and are declining globally due to accelerating threats from agricultural expansion, habitat loss, and climate change (Bowler 2021). Bee populations of all kinds are declining. The western bumblebee, once common on the CT, has declined 72 percent according to work by Janousek, Douglas, and Cannings (2023).

David Inouye, an ecologist with three decades of study at the Rocky Mountain Biological Laboratory near Crested Butte, states, "Already the difference in timing between seasonal events at low and high altitudes has negatively influenced migratory pollinators, such as hummingbirds, which overwinter at lower altitudes and latitudes" (Inouye 2020). "If climate change disturbs the timing between flowering and pollinators that overwinter in place, such as butterflies, bumblebees, flies, and even mosquitoes, the intimate relationships between plants and pollinators that have co-evolved over the past thousands of years will be irrevocably altered. As the climate changes, we're tending to get less snow and warmer and earlier springs. A paradoxical consequence is that we're getting more frost damage. The effects ripple through the ecosystem as global warming disrupts plants and seed production, which, in turn, means less food for small mammals and birds."

Interactions between broad-tailed hummingbirds and their food plants have been studied extensively in western Colorado, near the northern limit of the breeding range (Inouye 2000). At the Rocky Mountain Biological Lab near Crested Butte, territorial male and nesting female broad-tails forage for nectar at a series of herbaceous perennial plant species that flower in sequence through the summer. The earliest of these is the glacier lily, *Erythronium grandiflorum*, whose flowering begins about one week after snowmelt and ceases about two weeks later. The glacier lily is blooming 17 days earlier than 50 years ago, and the broad-tails have partially compensated by arriving 12 days earlier than they used to. Some wildflowers are blooming early but suffer and die from late frosts. Can all of the pollinators compensate too? *National Geographic* magazine has a revealing look at these problems (Welch 2023).

Some butterflies are in trouble too. The monarch butterfly used to be one of the most abundant and beloved species. Western monarchs have declined 99.9 percent since 1970. The significant problems afflicting western monarchs are habitat loss (overwintering and breeding areas), pesticide use (herbicides and insecticides), and climate change (including increased drought severity and frequency). Along the first hundred miles of the CT, the Platte River watershed is home to the similarly threatened Pawnee montane skipper.

On the western part of the CT is the endangered Uncompahgre fritillary butterfly's habitat, limited to eleven verified sites in the San Juan Mountains. All known populations are associated with large patches of snow willow above 12,000', which provide food and cover. This species is found primarily on northeast-facing slopes, which are the coolest and wettest microhabitat available in the San Juan Mountains. These are but a few of the rare endemic species with small existing habitats that are threatened by climate change and development in the Colorado mountains.

La Garita

From mile 391 to mile 405, the trail passes through the La Garita Wilderness, one of the original five wilderness areas designated in Colorado in the 1964 Wilderness Act. Overall, the La Garita straddles 35 mi. of the Continental Divide and 14 mi. of the Colorado Trail. On its eastern border is the Wheeler Geologic Area, originally a national monument, then rescinded, then excluded from a designation bill, but later restored to the La Garita Wilderness. Here volcanic tuff has been eroded into spires, columns, and flutes naked of any vegetation.

La Garita Caldera is a large super volcano caldera in the San Juan volcanic field in the San Juan Mountains near the town of Creede. The eruption that created the La Garita Caldera is among the largest-known volcanic eruptions in Earth's history, as well as being one of the most powerful known super volcanic events. The resulting Fish Canyon Tuff has a volume of approximately 1,200 cu. mi. By comparison, the eruption of Mount Saint Helens on May 18, 1980, was 0.25 cubic cu. mi. in volume. The San Juan Volcanic field was the source of the vast amounts of gold and silver produced in the Silverton–Creede–Lake City area in the late 1800s (Blair 1996). Hikers and tourists flock to see the old, abandoned mines and ghost towns in the area.

La Garita Wilderness is named for the Spanish word for "Lookout," as legend has it that Utes sent smoke signals from nearby 13,710' La Garita Peak. The trail passes conveniently by the near-14er 13,983' Stewart Peak, closely followed westward by 14,017' San Luis Peak, which I climbed on a previous Colorado Trail hike. It is a relatively easy 2 mi. hike up from the trail with outstanding view of the Los Pinos and Cebolla Creek drainages to the north and the majestic San Juans to the west. San Luis is named for Louis IX, the only French King to be canonized. As an example of the many places named for Louis—think also St. Louis. Views to the north show the fantastic horns and aretes of glacier peaks of the Uncompahgre Wilderness and the high tundra of the Powderhorn Wilderness.

The trail continued west to the Eddiesville trailhead. There is no town, just a road's end and private ranch. We saw a big tent canopy and hoped for trail magic, but no one was around. We had lunch with Lola and Hamilton, who had been leapfrogging us. Still hot, we climbed through the afternoon up to the headwaters in the subalpine and camped beneath dead spruce trees with Lola and Hamilton at about 11,500'. The mature spruce forest in the whole area is completely dead. It was very disturbing; my 2007 hike through this area did not show this level of mortality at all.

This stretch of the trail for the next hundred miles is some of the best lynx habitat in the state. Lynx are grayish and larger than bobcats (up to 30 lb.) and have long ear tufts and huge feet to power them through the deep snows of high elevations. Lynx are classified as threatened in Colorado despite a fifty-year reintroduction program (Colorado Parks and Wildlife 2014). Most of the 200 or so lynx in the state are found in the San Juan Mountains. They feed on snowshoe hare and the hare feed on bark and twigs of spruce and subalpine fir among other vegetation. The hare turn white in winter to camouflage them from their mortal enemy, the lynx. Lynx and snowshoe hare numbers tend to run in cycles; when prey numbers decline, lynx numbers decline. These dead forests are probably more lost habitat for hare and lynx in Colorado, and the already-tenuous lynx population may not survive climate change. I looked for cat scat along the trail but did not see any.

The wolverine is another similar-sized carnivore of the subalpine but is classified as an endangered species and is likely extinct in Colorado. The largest member of the weasel family, it is similar to the lynx in its habitat needs but different in its diet. Whereas lynx are dependent on the hare as prey, ferocious, powerful wolverines are reportedly able to bring down much larger prey, even moose, according to some accounts. Wolverines are notorious travelers, requiring hundreds of square miles and capable of traversing the roughest terrain with ease. Except for a very rare sighting in 2009 of a wandering Yellowstone wolverine, they were last seen and trapped out of northern Colorado more than a century ago. Colorado Parks and Wildlife is assessing whether to reintroduce this native predator. Wolverines need heavy snowfall environments for denning and hunting, and alas, climate change makes them unlikely to flourish if they are reintroduced. As long as the snows persist, the San Juan Mountains may be the best hope as ideal habitat for this rare species.

Just 10 mi. southeast of here is where John C. Frémont abandoned his 1848 disastrous winter San Juan Mountains expedition. Frémont, popularly known as "The Pathfinder" during his times, was considered an American hero. He was the first white man to penetrate these unmapped mountains. Although celebrated as an explorer, he was arrested and court-martialed by General Stephen W. Kearny during the Mexican-American War. In his fatal fourth western expedition, Frémont planned to follow the 38th parallel as closely as possible and locate a new pass over the Continental Divide in the vicinity of the Cochetopa Pass, which led out from the San Luis Valley and would open a route over the San Juan Mountains into the Valley of the Green River.

Although warned at Bent's Fort that the coming winter snows would make it impossible, he pushed on. Accordingly, scout Old Bill Williams led the party north up Alder Creek and into the San Juan Mountains, an impassable wintry waste where the snow was more than 10' deep and the temperature fell to −20°F. Somewhere in the snow Bill Williams lost his way, and the party turned north 15 mi. too soon. By the middle of December, they were

12,327' above sea level, on Pool Table Mesa near Wannamaker Creek, and caught in a heavy snowstorm.

After eating their mules, it was not until December 22 that Frémont acknowledged that the party needed to regroup and be resupplied. They began to make their way to Taos in the New Mexico Territory. By the time the last surviving member of the expedition made it to Taos on February 12, 1849, ten of the party had died. Except for the efforts of member Alexis Godey, another fifteen would have been lost. After recuperating in Taos, Frémont and only a few of the men left for California via an established southern trade route. In all, ten perished in a month-long ordeal before rescue. One man was cannibalized. A few years later in 1852, Army captain John Gunnison followed Frémont, chopping a route over Cochetopa Pass hoping to find a rail route to California, but a feasible route was stopped by the Black Canyon of the Gunnison. He pushed on to Utah, where he was killed by Paiutes.

I sometimes wish I had been born in the times the West was explored, to see it in its "naturalness," realizing that Native Americans were part of nature. Frémont was trained in the natural sciences and collected over twenty-five first species, which have been named in honor of him. As a naturalist and amateur botanist myself, I respect him for that and wish I had been on his expeditions, although this winter expedition would not have worked for me. I much prefer summer traveling.

Beetles and the Dead Forest

The trail was now entering vast forests of dead spruce trees. We had been seeing forest mortality since Monarch Pass, but it was becoming the norm here. In southwest Colorado, the spruce bark beetle epidemic started on Wolf Creek Pass in the late 1990s and with the drought really took off around 2004. Now, the beetles have worked west through the Weminuche Wilderness, north toward Silverton and Telluride. As of 2020, spruce beetles had torn through nearly 1 million acres of the Rio Grande and San Juan National Forests, which, combined, total about 3.6 million acres, though not all of that land is spruce forest. Western spruce budworms have devastated a similar acreage in southwest Colorado. The spruce beetle outbreak has currently affected approximately 40 percent of the San Juan National Forest's high-elevation forests, moving onto the forest from the east.

Bark beetles are native species, and infestations of this scale have happened before. What is different is that the Earth's climate is changing for the first time in thousands of years, making the scope of forest mortality difficult to predict. As I hiked, the dead forest deeply offended me at an aesthetic level but at a scientific level, beetle kills have been a normal part of a healthy forest when viewed over centuries. While beetles may cause ecosystem change, the opening of the canopy of dead forests stimulates growth of an understory of vegetation for pollinators and other wildlife. After a few years of regeneration of flowering plants and shrubs, dead forests support greater species richness of birds and bats than the original spruce forest. Bark beetle populations are stimulated by winter warming conditions, and host trees are more vulnerable to beetle kill when drought-stressed, as their defenses to flush invading beetles with sap are much reduced. Beetles, wildfire, and climate change are the trifecta of death that is killing our forests (Quresh et al. 2020).

A few young spruces are growing, and I hope they can survive the insect pests and climate change. The Forest Service has been doing salvage sales in dead forests, and resilience treatments in live spruce and aspen forests, as well as fuels reduction and prescribed burning. In 2020 reforestation projects on public lands showed high seedling mortality, a result of bone-dry conditions on the landscape, and a frost killed much of the cone crop. There is some disagreement and doubt among scientists that fuels reductions actually help reduce wildfire, especially in high-severity crown megafires and higher altitudes. They probably do help in low-to-moderate severity wildfires and at lower elevations. We can't pick and choose where or what severity of fire may occur in the future, but the simple truth is the less fuel, the less fire.

It is worth reminding that living subalpine forests collect and trap snowpack. Strong winter winds blow snow off the peaks into valleys, where trees collect and trap the snow by wind shear and friction. Spring snowpack is much deeper in the forest where it is shaded, so it melts more slowly. Dead forests may produce earlier and more overall stream flow but don't function as well to protect snowpack, and snowmelt runs off faster. Both ecosystems and human users need snowpack to melt slowly over the summer to keep soils moist and streams flowing, and to enable fish populations to survive.

Even in the absence of bark beetle outbreaks and wildfire, trees in Colorado subalpine forests are dying at increasing rates from warmer and drier summer conditions; according to recent University of Colorado Boulder research by Robert Andrus et al. (2021), 2018 was the warmest year in southwest Colorado in the last 124 years. Andrus says we have bark beetle outbreaks and wildfires that cause very obvious mortality of trees in Colorado. But his work is showing that even in the areas where people recreate and the forest looks healthy, mortality is increasing due to heat and dry conditions alone. Drought mortality may exceed bark beetle mortality more than threefold and, like bark beetles, affects the largest trees. And large trees sequester the most carbon. Andrus has also found that some regeneration of spruce is occurring after beetle kill, but forests suffering wildfire after spruce-beetle kill are not regenerating.

Hart, Andrus, Rodman, and Veblen have cooperatively published several papers on climate-related factors that are causing forest mortality in the subalpine zone (Veblen, Romme, and Regan 2012; Andrus et al. 2021; Rodman et al. 2022). They show that both summer drought and winter drought induce greater spruce-beetle-caused mortality. As the climate warms, snowpack is declining. Less snowpack translates to drier soils and stressed trees that are unable to fight off beetle attack. Less snowpack also increases wildfire hazard as living trees and vegetation lose moisture. Beetle outbreaks are strongly driven by climate, and there is little forest management can do to prevent them. Rodman has shown recent bark beetle outbreaks in subalpine forests of the Rocky Mountains have reduced tree size and altered species composition. Andrus and coauthors (2021) have shown a strong relationship between higher rates of tree mortality and warmer, drier summer climate conditions, implying that climate warming will continue to increase background mortality rates in subalpine forests. Increases in disturbances (like beetles and wildfire), combined with declining frequency of wetter and cooler years suitable for seedling establishment, are increasing subalpine tree mortality. While eventual recovery of the preoutbreak subalpine forest structure (tree size) is likely in most places, changes in species composition may persist for decades, favoring aspen and subalpine fir.

According to the Colorado State Forest Service (2020), over 22 percent of the standing trees in Colorado forests are deadwood. Most are killed by insects (65%), disease (23%), and fire (4%—this is a pre-2020 estimate before the megafires). Instead of sequestering carbon like a healthy forest does, the decomposing deadwood releases carbon into the air. Increasing drought further stresses trees. Trees defend themselves from bark beetle attack through a series of resin ducts and chemical compounds therein that they use to flood the beetles out through their boreholes. Precipitation has become more variable in recent years. With inadequate rain and snowfall, trees' ability to defend themselves from attack typically decreases, as available resin is reduced. For the ninth consecutive year, spruce beetles remained the most destructive forest pest in Colorado. Since 2000, this small, native bark beetle has affected a shocking 1.88 million cumulative acres of forest in our state.

Frosty, Grasshopper, and I have entered the San Juan Mountains. Nearly all of the landscape traversed by the trail in the San Juans was glaciated in several epochs, the most recent being the late Quaternary or Pleistocene geologic period, when large mammals like giant sloth, camels, ancestral bison, and saber-toothed cats roamed the state. But these animals did not reside in the San Juan Mountains. Most of the entire area—from Carson Peak on the east to Engineer Mountain on the west, to Lake City and Ridgeway on the north and Durango on the south—was covered in glaciers in the Pleistocene. The ice occurred to over 11,500', so many mountains and valleys were buried in ice, and only the tallest ones poked out as "nunataks." Ice covered over 1,000 sq. mi. and was over 3000' thick in Animas Canyon (Blair 1996).

The ice receded by 5,000–13,000 years ago, but the gravel outwash carried far downstream, leaving the magnificently carved mountains of the mighty San Juans. It must have taken thousands of years to build soil and develop the forests we have today. Glaciation left the high-mountain cirques often holding jewel-like lakes (63 in the Weminuche alone). Three 14ers grace the Weminuche Wilderness to the south of the trail—Windom Peak, Sunlight Peak, and Mount Eolus—as well as equally awesome summits in the Needle Mountains and Grenadier Mountains that are viewed from the trail. Several other 14ers are found in the San Juans.

We saw lots of pikas, those small hamster-like mammals that live in the rocky fell fields of the alpine. Pikas are vocal, with frequent chirps to warn of danger; often you hear them before you see them perched on rocks. They don't hibernate; they cut grasses during the summer and store them below snow underground as hay to feed on during the winter. Animals that live under the snow layer are called *subnivean*. Voles, pocket gophers, and mice are also subnivean. Biologists were concerned that pikas might be threatened by climate change because they have a narrow temperature tolerance and because there is nowhere for them to escape but uphill; they are already near the mountaintops. The good news is that recent data suggest they may be more resilient than anticipated.

The alpine tundra ecosystem climate is characterized by strong winter winds, extreme cold, abundant precipitation—mostly as snow—and short growing seasons. Much of the snow blows off the tundra during winter, so the available moisture to plants is much less and soils are colder. Plants hug the ground to avoid damaging, desiccating winds and to conserve heat. Amazingly, some wildflowers can emerge from melting snow in the late spring, like glacier lilies, marsh marigolds, and globeflowers.

Christy McCain (McCain, King, and Szewczyk 2021) studied how forty-seven small mammal elevational ranges have changed from their historical distributions (1886–1979) to their contemporary distributions (post-2005) along elevational gradients in the Front Range and San Juan Mountains of Colorado. Historical elevational ranges were based on museum specimens and publication records. Contemporary elevational ranges were based on thousands of records from systematic sampling efforts and museum specimen records. Of the mammal ranges, 26 changed upward, 6 did not change, 11 changed downward, and 4 were extirpated locally. The average range shift was 400' upward, while exclusively montane species shifted upward more often (75%) and displayed larger average range shifts. For species living at higher elevations already, such as the golden-mantled ground squirrel and the Uinta chipmunk, the shift was even more extreme: on average, those animals saw a 1,135' upward shift in elevation. She found the variables that best predicted upper limit and total directional change were species having a higher maximum latitude in its geographic range and montane affiliation, and the study mountain being at the southern edge of its geographic range. Thus, mammals in the Southern Rocky Mountains serve as harbingers of more changes to come, particularly for montane, cold-adapted species in the southern portion of their ranges.

The white-tailed ptarmigan is another alpine species threatened by climate change. It is the only bird to change to white plumage, its evolutionary adaptation to winter snow in its habitat to camouflage it from predators and possibly to add warmth. It has feathery tufts between its toes to act as mini-snowshoes. Ptarmigan feed on willow buds in winter and can shelter under the snow in storms. As snow cover recedes, will they be caught in white clothes when the tundra is bare? We did not see ptarmigan on the CT, but they are there. In summer, they are mottled brown and almost invisible unless they move. I have seen them many times before on high mountain slopes in Colorado. A related grouse we did see is the blue grouse, recently renamed the *dusky grouse*, which inhabits conifer forests. These grouse either explode in a huge whirr almost underfoot, or casually walk away.

I was lucky to see a pine marten hunting the fell fields, darting and weaving in and among boulders looking for pika and other rodents or ptarmigan. This larger member of the weasel family is commonly an arboreal (tree) species that hunts squirrels but will also hunt in the alpine.

Thinking about these vulnerable alpine communities makes one wonder about actual warming occurring on the ground. According to the Mountain Studies Institute (2012), southwestern Colorado warmed about 2.0°F in the period from 1977 to 2007. This rate of warming is the same as for western Colorado but greater than for the western United States, or any other region of the United States except Alaska. They say temperatures are likely to increase by an *additional* 1.5°F to 3.5°F by 2025 and 2.5°F to 5.5°F by 2050. On this trajectory, the increase at the time of writing equals or exceeds 4°F.

This rate of warming is almost double the worldwide increase of about 1.1°C or 2°F. To put this in perspective, consider the Paris Agreement of 2015. It was a legally binding international treaty on climate change. Its overarching goal was to pursue efforts to limit the temperature increase to 1.5°C above the preindustrial level. The most recent scientific Intergovernmental Panel on Climate Change (2023) finds that there is a more than 50 percent chance that global temperature rise will reach or surpass 1.5°C (2.7°F) between 2021 and 2040 across studied scenarios, and under a high-emissions pathway; specifically, the world may hit this threshold even sooner—between 2018 and 2037. We can double all these numbers for southwest Colorado, and ecosystem and hydrologic changes are happening there rapidly right now.

We hiked to 12,360' San Luis Pass on a gorgeous sunny day of alpine hiking and exited south to the Equity Mine, where Frosty's friend Terry took us to Creede for rest and resupply.

When I go to town, there are "chores" of eating, picking up my food box or shopping, finding lodging, taking a shower, washing clothes, and charging electronics. Oh, and eating some more! I will also call home and catch up on the news. Today was different, though. Anne met us in Creede with our resupply boxes. It was so good to see her! She snuck up on us while we were waiting in line at Kip's Grill and tried to see if I would notice her, and I did! We had good meals and toured Creede and the mining museum.

In 1890, the Upper Rio Grande Valley's destiny changed dramatically. Nicholas C. Creede discovered a high-grade silver vein on Willow Creek, a tributary of the Rio Grande. The great rush was on! The boom camp's population quickly swelled to 10,000. (There are about 850 full-time residents in Mineral County today.) Slab cities and tent towns like North Creede, East Creede, String Town, Jimtown, and Amethyst seemed to appear overnight. Fortunes were extracted from mines with colorful names such as Amethyst, Holy Moses, Commodore, Last Chance, and Kentucky Belle.

The weather in Creede was cloudy and drizzly, and the forecast for the mountains was for more rain. I found a waterproof pack cover in an outfitter shop and bought it. I should explain my rain strategy: I always carry a rain jacket with hood. I also bring an umbrella, which keeps the cold rain off my head and torso. Typical rain temperature at high altitude is near freezing, and it can sleet or even snow in midsummer. I was also carrying an emergency poncho to cover my backpack. Finally, I use a waterproof inner liner in my pack to keep its contents dry. In the high Colorado mountains, if your warm clothing and sleeping bag get wet, you can develop hypothermia and could be in real trouble. I also prefer nonwaterproof trail runners because waterproof boots or shoes will get wet in the intense rain, and they won't dry for days.

As a booming mining camp with money, Creede attracted notorious outlaws. One of these was confidence man Jefferson Randolph "Soapy" Smith. Soapy became the uncrowned king of Creede's criminal underworld and opened the Orleans Club. In my travels, I encountered stories of Soapy in other mining camps of the West, including Skagway, Alaska, where he was later killed in 1898. Other famous people in Creede were Robert Ford (the man who killed outlaw Jesse James), Bat Masterson, and William Sidney "Cap" Light (the first deputy sheriff in Creede, and brother-in-law of Soapy Smith). On June 5, 1892, a fire destroyed most of the business district. Three days later, on June 8, Ed O'Kelley walked into Robert Ford's makeshift tent saloon and shot him dead.

Hard rock mining continued as the dominant economic factor in Creede for nearly a century. In 1985, when the price of silver dropped again, the last mine, the Homestake, closed permanently. Today "Mineral County" is returning to its tourism roots. And Creede, the little mining camp that refused to die, shares not only its beautiful natural setting but also its colorful heritage with thousands of visitors every year. So much so, that, even trying for advance reservations, we could not find a hotel in town and had to stay in South Fork.

Even in the nineteenth century, the environmental damage done by mining in the Colorado Rockies was breathtaking. Many forests were clear-cut to support the mining, leading to our even-age overly dense forests of today. The timbers were used to shore up the mines or make charcoal to smelt the ore or wood for heating. Mine tailings still pollute the streams. Acid mine drainage still flows from old mine adits, and recently the Gold King spill of 2015 caused by the EPA made the Animas River turn yellow for a hundred miles downstream into New Mexico. Colorado is home to various Superfund sites that are abandoned mines, and land managers are trying to deal with the safety and chemical hazards of thousands of abandoned mines in Colorado. In my work with BLM, I helped investigate and remediate many abandoned mine sites, including those near Silverton. Colorado Trail hikers pass through some mining areas and although open mine shafts and other hazards are of historical value, hikers need to be alert to them.

7

Creede to Silverton

The Alpine Zone

Grasshopper Moves On

July had turned to August while we were in Creede, and it was time to return to the trail. I had breakfast and Anne drove us to Creede, where Terry drove us back to the trailhead. Most of the next hundred miles are in the alpine zone, above treeline to over 13,000'. The woody plants are limited to shrubby spruce and willow. This area can be dangerous during monsoonal thunderstorms, with lightning and potential hypothermia. It is also incredibly beautiful: there are long views of big peaks and grassy tundra studded with midseason wildflowers, woolly thistle, alpine avens, sky pilots, alpine forget-me-nots, old man of the mountain flowers in drier areas; and king's crowns and parry primroses, little red elephants, tall chiming bells, and various paintbrush species in wetter areas, to name a few.

Alpine plants are adapted to this harsh climate zone with short growing seasons because strong winter winds damage plants in the winter and desiccate them in summer. Physical adaptations make them low-growing (cushion or crevice) plants, nearer the warmer ground and out of the wind. Moss campion is the prototype cushion plant. Leaves are often more succulent or hairy to conserve moisture and warmth. Chemically, they produce red anthocyanin pigments in the spring that convert sunlight to heat to warm plant tissues. Most alpine plants can begin growing from carbohydrates stored in last summer's roots and begin to photosynthesize above 32°F to extend their growing season. Alpine plants are fragile and easily trampled; recovery can take decades. Hikers must stay on-trail and step on rocks as much as possible. For an exquisite read on alpine plants see Ann Zwinger and Beatrice Willard's treatise *Land above the Trees* (1972).

A recent Forest Service report found the alpine tundra to have high vulnerability to climate change (Rice 2020). In this ecosystem, the year-round temperatures are cold, the growing season is short, and high winds can dry out the soil and plants. Temperatures and moisture levels can change significantly over short distances. Despite these conditions—and also because of them—these ecosystems have a rich mixture of plant and animal diversity: low perennial grasses and sedges give way to mat-forming forbs, which support voles, pikas, and marmots, along with elk, bighorn sheep, hummingbirds, and butterflies during the short summer season.

However, these areas are slow to recover from disturbances such as road and trail building, water and wind erosion, fire, and trampling from recreation. Pikas, birds, and animals that molt (like ptarmigan), and plant communities in these ecosystems, are considered highly vulnerable to disturbance and climate change. And since they are often found in unconnected mountaintop locations, plant and animal migration potential is limited. In the meantime, these ecosystems may be subject to tree encroachment from lower elevations.

Climate-related tree encroachment into the alpine is being actively studied around the world. One study for the San Juan National Forest in 2012 found a modest upward movement of base treeline since 1951, and a 12 percent increase in tree density, at and below treeline, during this same time period. Although treeline had not changed significantly, the rate of growth had increased. The accelerated growth rate was evident in the stunted trees (*krummholz*) at treeline as well as young trees that were cored. Nearly all of the krummholz had bolted, mostly within the last fifteen to fifty years. Of the seven cores that they examined, all of them exhibited an increased growth rate after 1996, correlating closely with an increase in summer temperatures recorded at the Red Mountain Pass (Formica, Farrer, and W. Ashton 2014).

We hiked back up to San Luis Pass to return to the trail and then over two high saddles. We began up the highest third pass and hustled, trying to beat coming bad weather. I had been expecting rain from the annual monsoon, and it was really brewing this day. I donned all my rain gear and secured my pack with the pack cover and poncho. The temperature dropped as we climbed up into the rocky pass toward Snow Mesa, and it started raining midday. It rained for four hours, mixed with strong wind. The deluge was pretty intense near the top of our climb, at 12,550', and sight was limited to about a hundred yards. Grasshopper was out ahead beyond view, and Frosty was somewhere in the back. I was hurrying to try to get off the exposed area in case of lightning. My hands were cold holding my umbrella and trekking poles. I had rubber gloves in my pack but didn't want to wrestle them out and get everything wetter.

I caught Brian the Bishop (aka Litebrite) in the pouring rain. Litebrite was a trail name for the rainbow-speckled sit pad he carried strapped to the outside of his pack. It resembled the children's toy. I asked if he was doing okay, as I, myself, was getting wet and a bit hypothermic. He stared dully at me for a moment with water dripping down his face and said he was cold. There was no place to shelter and nothing to do but go on and keep generating body heat from moving.

We arrived at the edge of Snow Mesa, where Grasshopper had stopped. The rain had let up some, and we waited for Frosty. I was concerned about him with the weather and anxiously watched back down the trail for him. He soon caught up, and we took a short break. I have a memorable photograph of Frosty with his bright red rain jacket, rain skirt, and face and white beard wet and dripping. I thought we might tent up since we had met our mileage for the day. We were all wet and cold. There weren't really any sheltered campsites on Snow Mesa, so we decided to push on.

Snow Mesa is a 3 mi. long, flattish, treeless, high-altitude mesa over 12,000'. The Mesa is immense landscape, over 20 sq. mi. above 12,000'. Twenty years ago, when I hiked through here, over 1,000 head of sheep grazed the Mesa. Sheep grazing in the San Juans has been going on for over 100 years. After mining, it was the main economic use of these public lands. According to the *Durango Herald*, over 200,000 sheep used to graze in the San Juans (Romero 2016). The Forest Service says only about 6,000 graze throughout the San Juans now, mainly in the Weminuche Wilderness. Andrew Gulliford (2021) cites as many as 369,000 sheep in the San Juans in the early 1900s; sheep hooves cause damage to the humus and soils, which were exposed to the drying sun, wind, and air and were washed down into the creek bottoms with the first heavy rains.

With the reduction in sheep grazing and warming, willow shrubs are encroaching into many herbaceous-dominated communities in alpine tundra in Colorado. Researchers on Niwot Ridge examined willow cover changes from 1946 to 2008 at alpine tundra in Colorado using aerial photographs (Scharnagl, Johnson, and Ebert-May 2020). This area had intensive sheep grazing prior to the late 1940s. They linked this pattern of change with experimental assessment of the effects of increasing summer temperatures, winter precipitation, and nitrogen deposition from air pollution—factors that this region has experienced over this period—on willow growth and survival. Shrub cover expanded by 441 percent over sixty-two years and is increasing at an exponential rate, corresponding to increases in carbon storage. Nitrogen and temperature facilitated willow growth, and snow increases survival. The researchers found clonal growth accounted for more expansion than seed dispersal and that shrubs have expanded into wet, moist, and dry meadows. In addition to a release from grazing, they suggest that global change could be driving shrub expansion.

Domestic sheep carry a pathogen that, when transmitted to bighorn sheep, causes deadly pneumonia in bighorns and reduces lamb survival rates for years. The pathogen—known as *Mycoplasma ovipneumoniae*—is especially deadly because bighorns and domestic sheep are mutually attracted to each other. Once disease is in a bighorn herd, members of that herd can easily transmit the disease to nearby herds. There is no cure or vaccine. Bighorns coming into contact with sheep are killed by state biologists to prevent spread of the disease to the bighorn herd. The Forest Service tries to manage sheep in non-bighorn-herd areas, but it is nearly impossible to do, as the bighorn roam freely. Plus, sheep often wander off their allotment.

There are four bighorn herds near the new allotment in and around San Luis Peak. These four herds interact to form the larger Central San Juan bighorn metapopulation. There are also three other bighorn populations within easy traveling distance for a bighorn, including the Weminuche population to the south, the Natural Arch / Carnero population to the east, and the San Juan West population to the west.

The Forest Service has apparently retired the Snow Mesa sheep allotment, as we did not see any sheep here. I learned later they have replaced it with another allotment in the alpine area near Creede. (Although we did not see sheep there either, we could smell them and did see scat.) This new domestic sheep allotment was created after the Forest Service determined domestic sheep grazing in the adjacent Snow Mesa area placed bighorns at too high of a risk.

Bighorn sheep were wiped out during the era of western settlement, as nonnative pathogens carried by domestic sheep were transmitted to native bighorn sheep. By the early 1900s, bighorns had vanished from several states, with only a few thousand remaining from an estimated historic population of 1.5 to 2 million. Following more than six decades of extensive and costly restoration efforts, bighorn sheep have now been recovered to only 5 percent of their historic population levels and exist on roughly 10 percent of their historic range.

We ended up hiking the muddy trail all the way down to forested Spring Creek Pass. We stayed relatively dry except for our shoes and socks. There was trail magic here, so we set up camp nearby. It was cold and damp but not raining. We were all pretty tired after 15 mi. at high altitude and the rain. I was thankful my gear stayed dry. That evening, I was concerned about the next day's weather and where we would camp.

Many CT hikers take a resupply break at Lake City. Another old mining town, Lake City was incorporated in 1873. Nearby is the site of the Alferd Packer Massacre Site, where Packer's party got stranded in the winter of 1874 and the party cannibalized one another until only Packer survived and was later sent to prison. With the completion of the first road into the mountains in this region, Lake City served as a supply center for the many miners and prospectors flooding into the area. As a supply center, the town boomed to as many as 3,000 to 5,000 settlers. But as the first-discovered deposits were found to be only moderately productive and no new extensive or rich deposits of minerals were found, by 1879 the boom had subsided. With the arrival of the Denver and Rio Grande Railroad in 1889, Lake City saw a second upturn in the economy that lasted into the 1890s. The railroad cut the cost of shipping gold and silver ores to smelters, reduced the cost of shipping supplies into Lake City, and provided shipment of cattle and sheep into the area for summer grazing in the high alpine meadows. Today Lake City is a quaint touristy town peopled by Texans and their 4WD vehicles. Nonetheless, it is in a spectacular part of Colorado.

It was cloudy in the morning and had drizzled the night before. I packed a wet tent and headed out. We had about an hour of sun hiking across treeless, stony Jarosa Mesa. I could smell sheep but did not see them. The mesa had very little vegetation, mostly cushion plants growing in the rock crevices, and appeared to be overgrazed. I was surprised to find myself over 12,000' on these gently rolling hills.

The trail here and for the next many miles is considered part of the La Garita Stock Driveway. Historically, it was used to drive livestock, especially sheep, to the high country. Grazing permittees continue to use it during the summer. About 1916, the Stock-Raising Homestead Act encouraged sheep ranching in western Colorado, and Basque herders from France and Spain immigrated to settle this area, bringing huge sheep herds to graze on then-unregulated public lands. As previously mentioned, this section of trail is a legacy of sheep raising on the high alpine tundra. At lower elevations, cattle-men warred with sheep men over access to public lands. Overgrazing ensued, and the government responded with the Taylor Grazing Act and began to regulate grazing. It's hard to imagine what the country was like before then. Of course, it is still beautiful, but has it been restored or is it still damaged? Is it naturally grassland or shrubland?

Back on the trail, it started raining about 10 a.m. We pulled into an area where there was a supposed yurt with a supposed spring, but there was no yurt nor spring. We needed water for the next 10 mi. alpine traverse over the CT high point. As we rested, Grasshopper thrashed through wet willows looking for water, but I found an easier source.

I decided to tent here and wait on the weather. Frosty and a couple of other hikers did too. Grasshopper and Brian, the State Episcopal Bishop from Mississippi, wanted to go on. They said they would wait up for us the next day. The next few miles' climb to the CT highpoint was over 13,000', so I decided the prudent thing was to wait for better weather—the next morning if necessary.

The weather improved in later afternoon, and Frosty and I decided to hike a few more miles. It grew sunny before sunset, and we were facing a 500' climb to 13,000'. We camped on the tundra near the headwaters of Ruby Creek and got our wet things dry! At least for a while until it really poured from 6 to 9 p.m. We had made a good decision to stop where we did. We were treated to celestial fireworks but none too close. I saw fabulous arcing rainbows out of my vestibule. Once again, with closed tent doors, my tent had ice condensation in the morning and it was 32°F.

The Fountain in the Sky

An overlooked area for wilderness designation, the Carson Peak Roadless Area is also an important wildlife and plant corridor linking the San Juan with mountain ranges to the north along the Divide. The area contains fifteen miles along the Divide. The Colorado Trail and CDT tightrope the Divide here with miles of fine alpine tundra hiking. Nearby Carson Peak is a high point near the trail and is easily climbed, at 13,657'. To the north lie 14er Handies Peak, American Basin, and the headwaters of the Gunnison River, and to the west, headwaters of the Animas River—both important water basins of the Colorado River. To the south lies the headwaters of the Rio Grande River. This area is truly a vast water fountain in the sky for the ecosystems nestled around it and is of critical importance for millions of downstream human users.

As the climate changes, the mountain snowpack melts off much faster, with a myriad of consequences. Flooding is only one of them. The landscape dries out quickly and becomes much more fire prone, extending the fire season by months. Biodiversity is threatened as scientists say we are in the sixth mass extinction, this one by human-caused climate change and land use (Kolbert 2014). Streamflows decline and warm, threatening trout fisheries, especially for cutthroat trout, who require maximum daily temperatures near the optimum growth temperature of about 57°F. Wildfire and drought reduce shading of streams, and warming air temperatures are a threat to cutthroats, who are more sensitive than nonnative trout like brook trout and rainbow trout.

The increasing average temperatures are reducing stream flows; every 1°F rise in temperature equates to a 3–5.2 percent reduction in stream flows, according to Andy Mueller (n.d.) of the Colorado River Water Conservation District. With the current 4°F increase, that equals a 12–21 percent reduction in streamflow. Timing of runoff adds to the problem; water managers can't store all the early flush of water in reservoirs, and some is lost downstream.

Another consequence has to do with albedo, the amount of solar radiation reflected from the ground surface.

In a recent paper in the prestigious journal *Science*, P. C. D. Milly and K. A. Dunne (2020) estimate that mean annual Colorado River discharge has been decreasing by 9.3 percent per °C of warming because of increased evapotranspiration, mainly driven by snow loss and a consequent decrease in reflection of solar radiation. Up to half of the drop in the Colorado River's average annual flow since 2000 has been driven by warmer temperatures, four recent studies found. They have concluded that much of this climate-induced decline—amounting to 1.5 billion tons of missing water, equal to the annual water consumption of more than 10 million Americans—comes from the earlier shrinking and melting of the region's snowpack. Fewer days of less snow means less heat is reflected from the sun, causing warming of the ground, air, and water, creating the albedo effect. Studies by Mu Xiao, Bradley Udall, and Dennis P. Lettenmaier (2018) show that pervasive warming has reduced snowpacks and enhanced evapotranspiration over the last 100 years; over half (53%) of the long-term decreasing runoff trend is associated with the general warming.

The Colorado River serves 40 million people in seven states and Mexico and much of our country's agriculture. In 2023, federal officials declared an emergency water shortage on the Colorado River for the first time. The shortage declaration forces reductions in water deliveries to specific states, beginning with the abrupt cutoff of nearly one-fifth of Arizona's supply from the river, and modest cuts for Nevada and Mexico, with more negotiations and cuts to follow. The river is overappropriated based on a 1920s climate that was wetter and cooler and planning that did not factor in megadrought. The changing climate is already affecting everyone in the West by delivering more catastrophic wildfires, more unhealthy smoke, less water, and higher agriculture prices.

Recent work by Erica Siirila-Woodburn and others (2021) has found that across the western United States, snow-water equivalent declines of about 25 percent are expected by 2050. (Snow-water equivalent is the amount of water in the snowpack.) The Mountain West has already lost 20 percent of its snowpack since the 1950s and could lose another 50 percent by the end of the century. There is less consensus on the time horizon of snow disappearance, but model projections combined with a new low-to-no-snow definition suggest about thirty to sixty years before low-to-no snow becomes persistent if greenhouse gas emissions continue unabated. In the upper Colorado River basin, they predict *low-to-no snow for 50 percent of the basin by 2050* and 75 percent by 2062. Diminished and more ephemeral snowpacks that melt earlier will drastically alter groundwater and streamflow dynamics.

The big picture inescapable conclusion is that we have impaired our planet's climate cycles, and our burgeoning population and fossil fuel-powered lifestyle have exceeded the water-carrying capacity of the basin and the planet.

Monsoon

Another hard day, and the weather did not cooperate. We left early at 6 a.m. to climb a long ridge for the big 6 mi. traverse over 13,000'. The weather during the monsoon is most stable early until about 10 a.m. In a Zen-like moment, I watched the sunrise and sunbeams amid floating fogbanks below from the summit of an unnamed peak, at 13,000'. "He climbed cathedral mountains, he saw silver clouds below, saw everything as far as you can see," sang John Denver. We marched through the early morning, the sun at our backs and our long shadows playing out ahead of us.

We had nice aerial views of Lake San Cristobal and the Lake Fork of the Gunnison River. The lake was formed about 700 years ago when the massive Slumgullion Slide, a mass wasting earthflow, collapsed down the mountain to dam the river. The slide area was visible from our viewpoint as partly forested, partly barren yellow soils. I bet the Utes were surprised when it happened.

We traversed the long, high, grassy ridge with fine views interspersed with hanging clouds. Later, we reached the CT high point, a 13,286' grassy hump near Coney Summit. Coney is another name for pika. Frosty and I stopped at the commemorative sign for a break and photos. We finished the traverse and around 10 a.m. arrived at Carson Saddle, at 12,360'. Around here are abandoned mines, waste rock dumps, and shafts and a 4WD road. North of here is the old mining camp and the ghost town of Carson. Hiking on, we then encountered two midday storms with only an hour of no rain. We saw three moose down below us in the willows.

We almost cleared the next big pass, but it rained, then briefly cleared as I summited. Clouds became sun as we descended to Little Cataract Lake. This is a new route for me, as my previous hike led down beautiful Pole Creek (unfortunately, it now allows dirt bikes).

Frosty and I decided to camp here, as the next few miles over a big hill didn't appear to have camping and the weather looked like more rain. Of course, it started raining as we set up our tents. We've been having significant tent condensation problems because it rains every night; tent flaps are closed and insensible water loss from our breathing and skin for twelve hours amounts to about 1/3 l and makes the tents wet inside. I remember one night on the CDT, I was sleeping in my so-called breathable bivy sac and awakened to find snow between my down sleeping bag and the bivy sac! I could have made a large snowball from the amount in my bivy sack. Most nights, I leave my tent flaps open to let the condensation out.

It rained five times this day and again during dinner. We are behind schedule, wet, and tired of the rain and have decided to take the Stony Pass Alternate as a shortcut. No sign of Grasshopper and the Bishop.

Although I complain about the rain as a hiker, don't think a decent 2021 monsoon is the solution to the long-term drying of the landscape. I need to point out that the yearly snowpack is the real key to adequate water resources for ecosystems and humans. About 75 percent of the water used in the western US comes from snowmelt. Monsoons help the higher-elevation ecosystems in the summer like wildflowers, but the typical heavy rain / fast runoff does not soak into the soil nor recharge groundwater as melting snow does, and much is lost to evaporation. Nearby valley ranchlands did not see much monsoonal rain.

I woke up to a frosty tent again. It was 32°F at about 6:30 a.m. I shook out the ice from my tent and packed up. We headed out to the first of six hills to climb. Great weather for a change! The hills were tough and unrelenting, but the scenery was spectacular: Red Mountain, Vestal Peak, and The Guardian on the horizon.

We hiked all day long on alpine tundra over easy hills. I saw pretty monkeyflowers blooming near creeklets. Frosty randomly met a friend, Ric, whom he had worked with at ConocoPhillips. Ric was hiking with his son. The day's highlight was crossing through a band of about 500 curious sheep in a high alpine meadow. There was no herder nor were there sheep guard dogs. This area is part of a massive sheep allotment in the Weminuche Wilderness. Despite the surprise and fascination of seeing the free-roaming sheep here, I know they are a threat to our bighorn sheep and that domestic sheep don't belong here. When wolves are introduced to the Western Slope, sheep present an unnecessary temptation; predation and conflict will follow.

We continued to Stony Pass Road and hiked up to the summit, at 12,592'. Hard to believe, but this pass served as a supply route to the mines in Silverton and as the route to ship high grade ore out. On the Silverton side, it is a rough, steep, switchbacky road with some cliffs. I have read that outlaws would sometimes ambush the ore wagons, even though they were guarded. This road is only passable for a few months of the year and requires a lot of maintenance to keep open.

From here, meltwater flows into two mighty watersheds: southeast into the Rio Grande River and on to Mexico. Looking north, we can see that meltwater flows to the Animas River and on to the Colorado River, Mexico, and into the Sea of Cortez. Frosty was not feeling well, and we decided to take the CT Stony Pass Alternate, crossing the Continental Divide for the final time. It was six 4WD miles down to County Road 2 and 4 mi. more to Silverton. We hiked down a few miles into the forest, where an interesting guy named David offered a ride to town. David was giving his sister, a CT hiker, a ride back to the trail. There was still no sign of Grasshopper and the Bishop. We decided they must have continued on the official route into the Weminuche Wilderness.

The Weminuche

From mile 391 to 405, the trail passes through the beautiful, wild Weminuche Wilderness. At 492,418 acres, the Weminuche is the oldest and largest wilderness area in Colorado by twice. It occupies much of the San Juan Mountains and is the headwaters for the Rio Grande and San Juan Rivers. It was named after the Weminuche band of the Ute Mountain Utes. The usual suspects—miners, loggers, and Hinsdale County officials—opposed wilderness protection. The Weminuche elk herds survived extermination by hunters when the statewide population of elk had fallen to catastrophic levels around 1900. According to wilderness historian Mark Pearson (cited in Fielder and Fayhee 2002), its robust elk herds were part of the reason the state supported wilderness protection when it passed Congress in 1975.

Because of its size, remoteness, and plentiful prey, the Weminuche offers the last, best chance for survival of large carnivores such as grizzly bears, wolverines, gray wolves, and lynx. Unfortunately, grizzly bears, wolverines, and gray wolves are believed to be extinct in this area.

The last grizzly bear in Colorado was killed by an outfitter in 1979, also in the South San Juan Mountains. Supposedly, he killed the bear by stabbing him with an arrow while being mauled. The bear was an old female that apparently had never had offspring. Prior to that, the last grizzly was killed by a government trapper near Platoro in 1951 and declared extinct until the 1979 incident. While some harbor hope that a remnant ghost population still resides in the San Juans, grizzlies are likely gone from Colorado forever. David Petersen's *Ghost Grizzlies* (1998) gives an engrossing account of the search for them in the area. Other sightings have been reported since then but not documented by Colorado Parks and Wildlife. I have seen grizzlies from roadsides in Yellowstone, Glacier, and Alaska.

I have hiked nearly a thousand miles in grizzly habitat and seen tracks and scat but never seen one on the trail. Every minute I was alert and alive, not wanting to surprise a bear. Every night I took great care to prepare and store my food properly; I even used a bear fence in Montana on the Continental Divide Trail. I have actually met hikers who were attacked. On the CDT, a hiker friend, Smiley, was hiking near Brooks Lake, Wyoming. He surprised a sow with cubs on a curve in the trail. The sow attacked and, lacking bear spray, Smiley played dead and was badly bitten on the buttocks. Hiking alone, he was able to hobble back to a trailhead and get help. His injuries caused him to leave the trail for a few months, but he returned to finish late in the season. I always hoped, but also feared, seeing a grizzly at close range. There is something about not being the apex predator in the wild that makes your senses sharper and makes you more alive.

Recent work by Dave Mattson and Troy Merrill (2021) indicates that the San Juans are one complex in Colorado that could harbor a sustainable population of grizzlies. This is not surprising, since the area was the last redoubt of grizzlies in the state. The researchers state that successful restoration of grizzlies depends on the prospective lethality of humans. This is another phrase for social tolerance. Ecological traps occur when bears are lured into human-occupied areas by either human foods such as livestock or concentrations of high-quality natural foods such as fruit. The resulting inevitable conflicts typically lead to the deaths of involved bears. The San Juans harbor large bands of sheep on allotments on the alpine tundra, and the sheep would be a source of conflicts with the grizzlies.

Like the grizzly, the last native gray wolf born in Colorado was also killed in the South San Juan Mountains in 1945. Since then, rare dispersing individual wolves have been killed by cars or hunters in Colorado, but until recently, no known reproduction had occurred. Prospects for the gray wolf are improving with the recent arrival of a resident pack in North Park and with the 2020 ballot initiative requiring additional wolf reintroduction on the Western Slope. Already, ranchers are loudly complaining of the loss of a few animals in the winter of 2021–2022. Livestock killed by wolves can be compensated by the government. Ranchers want to take lethal control, but it is illegal to kill a wolf as wolves are classified as endangered in Colorado. Other means of protecting livestock exist like hazing, flagging (fladry), electric fences, and burros, but total protection is not practical for cattle on the range.

Recently, the Colorado Parks and Wildlife (2023a) released their final Wolf Restoration and Management Plan for comment. They propose releasing wolves in two areas: one circle with Aspen as an approximate center and another with Gunnison as a center. These areas were derived from work on the social tolerance of wolves based on the wolf reintroduction ballot initiative vote count and on the ecological suitability for wolves. They don't state how many wolves but do state populations from 50–150 statewide would be protected as endangered or threatened under state law. They suggest larger populations may be hunted. Conservationists are lobbying for larger numbers. Truly, the success of this plan will be subject to trial and error and, ultimately, to social tolerance.

Mountain lions occasionally take sheep and calves, although deer and elk are their main prey. Colorado is home to 3,000–5,500 mountain lions. Prior to 1965, there was a $50 bounty on lions, and the population dipped dangerously low. Colorado responded by halting the bounty but allowing sport hunting of lions, killing about 500 per year and planning recently to increase the percentage. Personally, I think mountain lions' ecological roles outweigh the importance of mountain lion sport hunting with hounds and not even using the meat (although probably some people use the meat). Mountain lions are increasingly coming into contact with people living in the wildland-urban interface as more people infringe on their habitat, and they are potentially dangerous to people. There have been twenty-three mountain lion attacks in Colorado and three fatalities reported since 1990. If you encounter a lion on the CT, don't run; stand tall, act dominant, and fight back with everything you have. People have actually killed attacking subadult lions with their bare hands.

As mentioned previously, Colorado Parks and Wildlife hatched a plan to kill hundreds of black bears and mountain lions in the Upper Arkansas watershed between Leadville and Salida and other parts of the state (Finley 2016). The rationale was to prop up declining mule deer herds, even though there is no scientific evidence that killing lions will increase herds. The reasons for decline are probably loss of habitat or drought. The plan was halted by a court decree in 2021 that prohibited the use of federal funds for the project because there had been no federal biological assessment.

Wolves and mountain lions are apex predators and keystone species, capable of beneficial ecosystem change by culling sick and weak prey and reducing artificially high deer, elk, and moose populations that are overgrazing their habitat. Scientists call this concept "trophic cascades." An apex predator is at the top of the food chain, and by culling herbivores (a lower trophic level), they stimulate vegetation, beaver, and insects (lower trophic levels). This in turn stimulates songbirds, fish, and many other animals. Overgrazing by elk and deer has destroyed riparian and other vegetation, causing habitat loss for birds, fish, and other small wildlife. The reintroduction of wolves into the Yellowstone ecosystem has reversed the overgrazing and overpopulation by elk there and restored riparian areas and wildlife species.

The Weminuche Wilderness is named for the Weenuchiu (preferred spelling) band of the Southern Ute Tribe. (Ouray was of the Tabeguache Ute Mountain Tribe.) Interestingly, Chief Ignacio, of the Weenuchiu, was able to hold onto reservation land in southwest Colorado near Towaoc and resisted the white man's land grab courtesy of the 1867 Dawes Allotment Act, a scheme that allowed reservation lands to be sold to non-Indians. This law has caused significant loss and fragmentation of reservation lands on the nearby Southern Ute Reservation and throughout Indian Country over the years. Other Ute bands from the Front Range and San Luis Valley were sent to the Southern Ute Reservation near Ignacio.

It was 1998 when my son Ryan and I made on our first trip into the Weminuche and the CT. We left the trailhead at Rio Grande Reservoir with a plan to hike to the Animas River. It was his first backpack. I did not even know about the CDT. We hiked up Weminuche Creek to Weminuche Pass, which is on the CDT, and headed west.

We would be backpacking for the next four days. As the clouds built up and grew dark, we continued heading west. As we descended into the forest it started to hail, covering the ground like snow. Since Ryan was small, I had brought an oversized one-man tent. I hurriedly set up our small tent, and we crammed in as the hail and the rain came down. I tried to assuage his discomfort with facts about how this was normal mountain weather.

As is often the case, the morning dawned clear, and we set out. We came to the 13,821' Rio Grande Pyramid and the "Window," an arch-like opening high on the mountain. At the pass, we passed a lone hiker, our first (and only). I asked, "Where are you coming from?" He said, "Canada." "Where are you going?" I asked. "Mexico," he said.

This guy was hiking the Continental Divide Trail when there were no markers, no phone apps, and only a confusing welter of maps. I had never heard of the CDT. Back in 1998, probably fewer than fifty people attempted a through-hike the trail. Dave Odell is the first hiker known to have hiked through the CDT, in 1977. These days, only about 200 or 300 people a year attempt to hike the entire trail, taking about six months to complete it.

I don't think I have been the same person ever since that chance meeting. Something kindled in me that would catch fire many years later when I would go on to hike the CDT myself.

On that bluebird day twenty-five years ago, my son and I continued west and hiked ten miles to above 12,000' and descended from the alpine to the Flint Lakes Area. Flint Lakes ranks up there on my beauty scale with Thousand Island Lake and Aloha Lake on the Pacific Crest Trail. These are high alpine lakes with stone islands, all very scenic with lush tundra and wildflowers beneath a cobalt sky. This is why I hike. Like the Utah explorer Everett Ruess, I admit I am a "vagabond for beauty," a phrase taken from the book of the same title by W. L. Rusho (1983).

We enjoyed our "nature fix." And the more time spent, and the wilder it is, the better the nature fix results. I suspect a component of nature is its raw beauty and peace and the appreciation it fosters for the plants and animals that are our natural legacy. At least those precious public places are left. In America, we are so fortunate to still have wild public lands in which to roam—entire landscapes of fantastic scenic beauty or community members as small as lupines, glacier lilies or Sierra lilies. . . . It will be forever our job to protect these places.

The next day, we fished at Ute Lake and we were fortunate enough to catch native cutthroat trout and admired their speckled beauty, marked with a red slash on their lower jaw (hence their name "cutthroat"). I released them as we did not bring any means to cook them.

Climate change also can affect fish communities such as native cutthroat trout through temperature changes that can affect growth and reproduction. The Colorado Natural Heritage Program studied both Colorado River cutthroat trout and Rio Grande cutthroat trout and rated them both "extremely vulnerable" to climate change. The rating is based on factors including barriers to movement and effects of warming stream temperatures that may impact cutthroat trout reproduction. These are the native backcountry trout that persist in high lakes and streams unaltered by the stocking of nonnative trout species. Invasion by nonnative brook trout is another major threat to our native cutthroats. This is part of our biodiversity heritage we need to protect.

We then hiked over Hunchback Pass and descended down to the old mining ghost town Beartown. There are no buildings left. The next day, we left the CDT in favor of the CT and hiked past pretty Kite Lake, crossed the pass and Divide, at 12,851', and looked down at beautiful El Dorado Lake on the left and an even more beautiful, unnamed lake on the right, both perched on opposing benches above the canyon. We descended the never-ending miles down Elk Creek to the Animas River trailhead at Elk Park, where we had arranged a pick-up on the Durango and Silverton Narrow Gauge Railroad. The train whistle blew and came into sight, brakes squeaking. We loaded our packs into a rail car and boarded the passenger car toward home. It was a momentous trip for me to share my love for the wilderness with my young son. On another day trip, I hiked east from Molas Pass to the Animas River and back. It is steep but has lovely old aspen forest, some of the best I have ever seen.

On another segment, in 2005, I hiked from Spring Creek Pass to Beartown. This southbound stretch for a hundred miles is a tightrope right on the high Divide. A friend, Nancy, hiked with me on this section and we started south on the trail. This segment differed from the current route by descending down lovely Pole Creek in the forest to the Rio Grande River near its headwaters, at 10,433', where we forded it. The Pole Creek drainage had aspen stands, lovely verdant meadows, and a rushing creek with a few tricky fords. I noticed dead aspens here and in other areas of southwestern Colorado. Researchers are attributing sudden aspen decline (SAD) to extreme drought and heat during 2002–2003 (Andrus et al. 2021). The trail has been rerouted along the Divide and, unfortunately, the beautiful Pole Creek trail now allows dirt bikes. More recently, Colorado has been in extended severe drought, and temperatures are rising with climate change. I hope our lovely aspen can weather the adversity.

Silverton

We accepted David's offer to drive us into Silverton. He is a young contractor working on aquatic assessments for BLM. David carefully drove Frosty and me the rest of the way down the steep, narrow, twisty Stony Pass Road and dropped us at the Silverton campground, where we were able to score a tent site. We walked a mile into town and had a great dinner at Handlebars. Silverton is an isolated mountain town, filled with nineteenth-century storefronts and boardwalks, old Victorian homes, mining museums, and lots of bars and restaurants for the barrage of summer tourists. It is a mecca for the jeeping and off-road vehicle communities, who love to explore the old mines and mining camps on rough mining roads. It is a great base camp for hiking the beautiful San Juans, and finally, the Durango and Silverton Narrow Gauge Railroad serves Silverton twice a day with thousands of day-visit tourists who have lunch, buy souvenirs, and return to Durango.

I visited Silverton several times as a boy with my family and years later with my own family. I have ridden the train as a boy and with my own children. I was fortunate to occasionally work in the area in my job, and I also took a *zero*, or rest day, here on my first Colorado Trail hike. As a trail town, Silverton is hard to beat. It offers lodging (expensive), campgrounds, restaurants and bars, laundry, gift shops, and mining museums—all within easy walking distance, with the mighty San Juans ringing the town. Yes, it gets congested when the trains arrive, but those visitors leave by later afternoon. And there are plenty of annoying jeeps and off-road vehicles around town.

As random coincidence so often happens on long trails, we met Frosty's friend Ric and son there, and they gave us a lift back to the campground. The next morning, we had breakfast back in town when Anne arrived. She gave us a lift back to our campsite. We washed clothes and showered while our wet tents dried in the sun.

Silverton lies in a high mountain Valley of the Animas River at 9,318', where harsh winters still isolate the town. When trespassing prospectors arrived to what is now Silverton, Ouray's Treaty of 1868 had officially established the area as Ute land. This authority did little to stop whites attracted by the mountains' mineral wealth. They explored the area in violation of the treaty, and by the early 1870s they made their way back to Baker's Park and the upper Animas River Valley. This activity led to the 1873 Brunot Agreement, also signed by Ouray, which ceded 3.7 million acres of the Ute Reservation for with the Ute Tribe was to receive $25,000 per year forever. This agreement officially opened the San Juans to white mining and settlement. Ouray was pressured into signing these treaties on the assurances that the whites would honor them. They did not.

The fate of Ouray's Tabeguache band who occupied lands in the Cochetopa Hills along the trail and nearby Powderhorn area was unfortunate after the Meeker Massacre at the White River Agency in 1879. Indian agent Nathan Meeker tried to force farming and Christianity on the Mountain Utes and plowed Indian lands without permission. At least forty-two army soldiers, Agent Meeker and agency personnel, and an unknown number of Ute warriors were killed. The "massacre" resulted from poor Indian Agency management and lack of promised treaty provisions. The Mountain Utes, including Ouray's Tabeguache band, were later exiled to a reservation in Utah near Ft. Duchesne. Colorado has a town and a mountain named after Meeker. Interesting how we honor genocidal men of the white invaders who unjustly treated Native or Black Americans. There are many such naming examples in Colorado and throughout the country.

Silverton's population soon doubled to 2,000. By 1885, the district's ore production reached $1 million per year, and in the 1890s it hit more than $2 million. From 1882 to 1918, the San Juan mining district produced more than $65 million in ores. The remains of scores of abandoned mines still litter the district and are an attraction to tourists and four-wheelers. Silverton and the Upper Animas Valley are still devoid of any forest, cut down to support the mines or poisoned by mine tailings, and it is not regenerating.

The Durango and Silverton Narrow Gauge Railroad still serves tourists visiting Silverton. In September 1880, William Jackson Palmer's Denver and

Rio Grande Railroad established Durango, and tracks reached Durango in July 1881. Almost immediately, workers started on the final 45 mi. stretch to Silverton, using parts of the Animas River wagon road for the railroad's route. The first train reached Silverton on July 8, 1882, traveling up the Animas River Canyon.

Later that day in town, we met the train on which Grasshopper and Brian the Bishop were arriving. They had decided Brian needed to see a doctor immediately and hopped off the train. Anne did a health assessment and offered to drive him directly to Durango to the hospital, and so Anne and I did. In retrospect, we should have had Frosty checked too.

We returned, and Grasshopper's friend Carla had arrived on the afternoon train and we met up for a nice dinner. Carla is about my age and had never done much backpacking, but she was fit and game for the adventure. We later learned Brian had a probable kidney issue but was OK to fly home. We had a nice couple of days' rest seeing the Silverton sights, mining museum, and old cemetery. In the 1880s, Silverton had thirty-four brothels along Blair Street, and prostitution was said to be the second-leading economic activity after mining. We found several headstones in the cemetery from the 1880s, marking graves of Silverton prostitutes as a "fallen woman" and "soiled dove." Often these unfortunate women were exploited and died from suicide or morphine overdoses.

About thirty air miles north of Silverton is the town of Paonia, home of the award-winning conservation publication *High Country News*. Its longtime publisher, Ed Marston, lost his life in 2018 to West Nile virus in a grueling fight. West Nile is transmitted by mosquitoes, and scientists have warned that West Nile cases are on the increase as the climate warms and dries, both in Colorado and the entire southwest. As the publisher of *High Country News*, Marston received the prestigious George Polk Award in Journalism in 1986 for the series Western Water Made Simple, which was later published as a book. In 1990, the University of Colorado Boulder awarded him its first Wallace Stegner Award "for faithfully and evocatively depicting the spirit of the American West."

Another giant of Colorado conservation and wilderness advocate is John Fielder, a renowned Coloradan photographer who trekked the Colorado Trail in 1990–1991 with pack llamas and young son JT "sherpa." Llamas helped him with his heavy photography gear and camping supplies. His beautiful photographs are contained in his book *Along the Colorado Trail* (1992) and were an inspiration to me to hike the trail. In 2006, and after John's prolonged caregiving for his wife's dementia, his son JT committed suicide backcountry skiing in the mountains the family loved. How much tragedy and beauty can a man take in his life? John has recently donated 5,000 of his priceless and best photos to History Colorado, the state's historical museum.

8

Silverton to Durango

More Alpine and Living Forest

Reunited but Frosty Falls III

An alpine area of high, craggy peaks, cliffs and horns, alpine lakes, and luxuriant wildflowers, the San Miguel Roadless Area has breathtaking scenery and a 20 mi. section of the Colorado Trail. Among its high peaks is San Miguel Peak, 13,752', and the beautiful Ice Lakes Basin. A forest fire in 1879 denuded the slopes west of Molas Pass, which have never recovered, but this area has some of the best wildflower gardens in the state. The San Miguel is not designated wilderness. According to Mark Pearson (Fielder and Pearson 2002), this failure at designation was primarily because of patented mining claims and foot-dragging by the Forest Service. Although its mountains are massive and sculpted, the area lacks 14ers and does not attract the hordes of peak-baggers, making it very attractive to hikers on the Colorado Trail.

Colorado senator Michael Bennet has championed the Colorado Outdoor Recreation and Economy Act, which was passed by the House and committees of the Senate as of 2021 but never became law. This would have included addition to several wilderness areas on the Western Slope and the 21,662-acre

Sheep Mountain Special Management Area, which contains the Ice Lakes Basin and the Cascade Creek portion on the Colorado Trail. This designation would protect it from mining and roads. We can hope it passes someday.

Anne drove us to Molas Pass, and we said goodbye. I have read Molas Pass may be the best place to see lynx based on multiple reports of motorists and backcountry travelers, especially in winter. It is a rare thrill to see a lynx; the only one I have ever seen was in Alaska. Unfortunately, because of a long-distance trail race in progress, there were too many people on the trail to see any wildlife.

We traversed the lovely upper Lime Creek Drainages. The trail race was underway, and we were passed by many runners. There are many creeks and open alpine country with many wildflowers. It is open because the Lime Creek wildfire of 1879 burned 26,000 acres. Very little forest regeneration has occurred in 143 years, a harbinger of the future if the subalpine areas burn. To our right were the hulks of Twin Sisters, 13,432', and Rolling Mountain, 13,696'.

It was a tough day for Frosty. He seemed good to go this morning at Molas Pass but grew weaker in the late morning with gastrointestinal issues. Grasshopper and Carla joined us at lunch, and Frosty discussed bailing. We were 10 mi. from the highway. There was a race aid station a mile ahead, so we decided to see if they had medical staff there to help decide whether he should continue.

Upon arriving, the station personnel had an EMT assess him, and we couldn't conclude a specific problem. But they had a larger aid station a few miles ahead with vehicles. Frosty decided to abandon the trail before getting deeper into the wilderness. The EMT had a radio, and I asked her to call ahead to secure a ride for Frosty back to town where he could meet his wife. Frosty had an inReach and texted his wife to meet him in Silverton. We hiked together partway, me carrying his heavy food bag. At the junction, I offered to hike down with him, but he waved me off and decided to hike the rest of the way himself. Although he seemed fully capable alone, I arranged the race sweep volunteer to accompany him. There were many other hikers and volunteers heading that way too. It was very sad for us all to see him leave after two weeks, but it was the prudent choice.

We continued over an unnamed pass, at 12,520'. The vistas to the north were outstanding, with partial views of the 14ers Mount Wilson, Wilson

Peak, and El Diente Peak, but the spire of Lizard Head commanded our attention. We descended the pass and hiked through towering *living* subalpine forest and thick foliage. We camped under live spruce near a babbling brook. Prior to here for the last hundred miles, all the high-altitude spruce forests had been dead via insect pests and drought. The peaks have changed to red sediments and conglomerate. Mushrooms were everywhere, indicators of a healthy mycorrhizal network.

Deer dug up the place I peed last night. They lick the salt from hiker urine to get minerals lacking in their diet. I was good to go at the appointed 7 a.m. time, but Grasshopper and Carla were not even close to being ready. Carla was chilled and was still warming up. Rather than stand around and get chilled myself, I hiked out slowly for 3 mi., stopping often to wait. Cascade Creek was beautiful and aptly named with several lovely waterfalls. After 3 mi., I waited 45 minutes. No one. I was getting worried, so I started hiking back the way I had come. After a quarter mile they showed up, a full hour behind. I was thankful nothing bad had happened.

Through the morning, we climbed over Sliderock Ridge, down into lovely Tincup Basin, and crossed the Bolam Pass jeep road. The trail continued a gentle climb west past the southern flank of Hermosa Peak, at 12,579'. Continuing on through a stately old-growth living spruce forest, we proceeded to Blackhawk Pass, where we ate lunch. Until the day before, we had not been in forest since before San Luis Pass. The forest north of there was mostly dead. We had since crossed over 60 mi. of alpine tundra and, south of Stony Pass, the forest was alive! Apparently, the bark beetles have not crossed the Divide here yet. I learned later that aerial survey mapping by the Colorado State Forest Service confirmed this.

During lunch on top of Blackhawk Pass, three trail runners and an older couple celebrating their fiftieth anniversary by through-hiking passed us. We had seen them back around Carson Saddle, many miles before. We continued into the Hermosa Special Management Area. Meaning "beautiful" in Spanish, Hermosa is an apt name for the colorful geology and luxuriant forest and tundra of the Hermosa Creek Drainage. Hermosa contains amazing diversity, with seventeen ecosystems. Its abundant water, plant diversity, lack of roads, and positioning along the Divide make Hermosa a critical wildlife and ecosystem corridor. Because of the living spruce forest, lynx are here. Old-growth uncut forests are found growing here at elevations lower than elsewhere in Colorado. Hermosa's colorful red shales and sandstones were laid down by marine deposits millions of years ago.

A late wilderness area addition, the Hermosa Creek was not designated until 2014 when signed by Barack Obama. The Colorado Trail traverses the western boundary of the wilderness for ten unforgettable miles of the Hermosa. On the left, wilderness. On the right, the special management area that preserves the area from new disturbances. A dozen mountain bikers caught us. It grew hot as we negotiated the final few hills to camp. The wildflowers were amazing, and we had much less smoke this day.

Indian Ridge

A big day. Beautiful weather, the kind of day you never forget. The route was easier this day, but we had a 13 mi. water carry. We marched all day as the day grew warm to Deer Creek, which was just a muddy trickle in heavy timber. It took me ten minutes to get 3 l. The water here was crucial, as there is no more water until over Indian Ridge to Taylor Lake. I had rain when I came through last time. Flowers were luxuriant, especially corn lilies, the medicinal osha (Porter's lovage), and, in full sun, thickets of tall pink tansy asters. For the entire hike, we have been seeing large 12–15" mushrooms, including the showy red with white splotches *Amanita muscaria*, also called fly agaric mushrooms. Magic mushrooms anybody? This mushroom is poisonous and hallucinogenic. Some people also confuse fly agaric mushrooms with psilocybin-containing mushrooms, but they are not the same. Surprise—this showy mushroom forms mycorrhizal networks with pine, spruce, and fir.

We also saw many brown-capped King Boletes the size of footballs that I found out later are quite edible and tasty. This mushroom can be found from 7,000' all the way up to treeline. They can be very abundant at higher elevations around 10,000'. They are typically on hillsides along streams under spruce trees. It's no surprise, *Boletus rubriceps* is connected in the soil with spruce roots via mycorrhizal fungus.

We camped just shy of the Overlook Trail as the anniversary couple was already there in a nice big campsite. Although there was room for us there, they weren't especially accommodating and we didn't want to crowd them. I walked out to the Overlook to a 270° mountainous panorama view to the north. Big climbs were on tap for the next day, but we had probably two more days to Durango.

The next day was also tough but spectacular. We had a long water carry and climbed south up and down five big alpine hills along Indian Trail Ridge with unending views around 12,000' with views into the Animas Valley. Along the way, we were side-hilling through lush fields of corn lilies, tansy asters, and sunflowers almost shoulder high. I saw a few western red columbines. At the top of the last big hill, we had a sudden steep, rocky, descent to beautiful, alpine Taylor Lake. We had had a 20 mi. water carry, so we rested and tanked up.

Here, the trail takes a big turn to the east toward Durango. There was a trailhead here and a Forest Service access road. There were a half dozen day hikers enjoying the scenery and rarified air. We could see barren hillsides to the east apparently from the 416 Fire in 2018. The views were outstanding, although it was hazy and partly cloudy. We crossed Kennebec Pass and had another steep descent down an impressive half-mile-long, talus field of shattered rocks. This seemed to be an ideal area for a rock glacier. Below treeline was an old-growth spruce forest with massive 4' diameter trees. That may sound small to East and West Coasters, but for Colorado that is as big as I have seen.

We leapfrogged with PikaBob, who had his tent chewed and invaded by pikas that stole a glove and a sock! There were thousands of cutleaf coneflowers, and monument plants (green gentians) as tall as I am crowded along the trail and creek.

After a rest, we descended another five mi. along the verdant riparian Flagler Fork, past a waterfall and on to the Junction Creek bridge. We passed 6' tall monument plants that may grow for sixty years before they bloom and sometimes bloom in mass unison. These plants and cutleaf coneflowers were everywhere with clouds of black and white Police Car moths tending them! These moths look like butterflies, lazily active in the full sunshine and having slender antennae. They seem to have no fear and allowed close approach, unlike butterflies.

No sooner had we set up camp than a half-dozen other long-distance hikers walked right into our camp! Space was limited here, so we shared in the spirit of the trail. I chatted with them about our respective experiences on the long trails. It was our last night on the trail. It was a 15 mi. day with 3,500' vertical gain and 5,600' descent for each of us, but Carla didn't complain a bit. I think she enjoyed her first long hike.

The other hikers camping nearby left early in the morning, and I didn't even hear them. After we broke camp, I led out for the climb out of the canyon and marveled at the steep, forested Junction Creek Canyon we sidehilled along. I reached the hilltop for great views and phone service to let family know I was well. Grasshopper and Carla caught up for a snack, and then I descended alone for many miles in a Zen-like mood down to Gudy's Rest, savoring the last day on the trail. I observed the life zones change before me as I descended from 9,600' to 7,000'. Spruce gave way to beautiful blueish white fir and healthy aspen more than 2' in diameter. Suddenly, Gambel oak and ponderosa pine dry forest took over as I descended and the day warmed.

A collaborative of land managers and nonprofit organizations called the Rocky Mountain Restoration Initiative (n.d.) has ambitious plans to treat lower-elevation forest for wildfire mitigation over hundreds of thousands of acres in the San Juan Mountains. I could not find any specific plans on their website, but I did find an awareness of the limitations of forest thinning and the benefits of prescribed fire.

I remember Gudy's Rest from my last hike, and it is truly a place of power, with commanding views over the Junction Creek Drainage and Animas Valley. Gudy Gaskill, of course, is the mother of the Colorado Trail. I had lunch, and Grasshopper and Carla caught up. After lunch, the trail rejoined Junction Creek, and we pushed on to the ending trailhead for photos. A hiker I had met ten days ago, Rainbow, had finished the day before and had a rental car. He was a trail angel and gave us a ride to Durango. I had been to Durango many times, but this was to be a short visit. We had a motel reservation, and, after a shower and a celebratory restaurant dinner, it was an early to bed.

Durango area's first encounter with white Europeans was the Domínguez-Escalante expedition, a Spanish journey of exploration conducted in 1776 by two Franciscan priests, Atanasio Domínguez and Silvestre Vélez de Escalante, to find an overland route from Santa Fe, New Mexico, to their Roman Catholic mission in Monterey. More than 100 years later, the Denver and Rio Grande Railroad Company helped form Durango along the banks of the Animas River to serve the San Juan mining district. Big strikes of silver (and later gold) were being discovered on Ute land in the mountains ever since gold fever had struck in 1872 and resulted in the settlement of mining town of Silverton, 45 mi. north. Despite the Treaty of 1868 giving the Utes ownership of the San Juans, because of the Meeker Massacre and general hatred of the whites for the Utes, Ouray was forced to give up millions of acres of these lands in the Brunot Agreement of 1873. Durango had a more tolerable climate and a good supply of water and coal for operating the smelters to pull precious metals out of the Silverton ore. Today, Durango is a bustling tourist mecca, the gateway to the towering San Juans and old mining camps via the Million Dollar Highway or via a narrow-gauge train.

The next morning, we enjoyed a big breakfast and Grasshopper and Carla gave me a ride back to my car on Monarch Pass, where we said goodbye. Reentry into society can be discombobulating. I seem to remember carefree early days of my life when the pace of life was not so frenetic; crime, social injustice, and gun violence were not so devastating; politics was not so polarized; and hot and cold wars were not so gut-wrenching. Nostalgia is clouding my perception. Of course, we had terrible assassinations, the Cuban missile crisis, the Vietnam War, terrible civil rights injustices that led to demonstrations, and other social injustices then too. All these are products of overpopulation, racism, pressure on limited resources, and clashing world views. We are all so electronically connected these days, yet it seems social media and cable media widen the gulf between Americans. The problems seem so intractable by inept or corrupt politicians concerned only with their own ego and winning the next election or war at all costs. They are less concerned about doing right by the public and the world as a whole.

I felt strong and alive after my hike but bittersweet at the same time. I felt refreshed and reconnected with my past and with the still-beautiful Colorado landscape. At the same time, I was saddened the trip was over, for leaving the serenity of the trail, for the sick and dying forests, and for friends who didn't finish or what might have been.

Epilogue

The Future of Colorado Forests

Hanging in the Balance

Despite the climate-induced changes in the landscape, the scenic beauty and serenity of the Colorado Trail still inspire a sense of wonder the second time around. This hike deepened my appreciation of the Colorado landscape but also brought into focus the crisis in its western ecosystems. Aldo Leopold famously said in my favorite book, *A Sand County Almanac* (1966, 225), "A thing is right when it tends to preserve the integrity, stability and beauty of the biotic community. It is wrong when it tends otherwise."

July 2023 has been named by the World Meteorological Society (2023) as the hottest month in the recorded history of the planet. Colorado has been in a multidecadal megadrought, the definition of climate change. Climate change is both wrong and an observable fact; it's just a matter of how serious it will get before our society truly confronts the threat. I fear our political environment is too reactionary—it won't respond until we are in irreversible crisis. Our handling of the pandemic is just another example of how our divisive politics gets in the way of solving problems.

If my hike was a vision quest, the vision is not pretty nor one that people want to hear.

Wildfire is a natural process of the forest, and small fires are healthy, reducing fuel loads and density of small trees, boosting the health of larger, reproducing trees, and opening wildlife habitat and increasing biodiversity. High-severity megafires are less natural and are becoming more frequent with unnatural tree density, more human disturbance, and a changing, drying climate. From my footsteps on the ground and travel to and from the trail, I can report that forest mortality from insects and drought has totally wiped out much of the high-altitude forest across much of the southwestern part of the state. A vast number of dead trees and fuels fill the forests. With very dry, windy conditions, dead fuels—and especially *living trees*—will burn with high severity, perhaps jumping the tundra as happened with the East Troublesome Fire. Wildfire has affected the lower montane eastern parts of the trail, but there are no new scars since my last hike and, overall, fire has so far spared most of the trail. Just last year, other regions of Colorado have suffered megafires unprecedented in recorded state history.

My hikes on the Pacific Crest Trail and Continental Divide Trail have led me through hundreds of miles of burned areas throughout the West. I fear for the future of our forests with continued drought, wildfire, and forest pests. We will see more drought, more beetles, more fire and longer fire seasons, more smoke, more dead forests, and more evacuations. Fire regimes and forest structure are changing. Veblen told me that in the coming decades our forests will likely decline in geographic area and constrict with altitude. Low-elevation forests will decline and give way to shrubland and grassland, and tundra above treeline is not likely to become forested, because of thin soil and climatic conditions. We may well see novel ecosystems emerge with a suite of species not typical of the historic "natural" ecosystems. Species are slowly marching northward in latitude. Our wildlife and forests need space to move and adjust to the changing climate.

Picture future southwestern forests with 4–6°F warming in our children's lifespans. Picture no snowpack. Yes, no snowpack. It's more than possible. On the current trajectory, in the high-altitude forest, some aspen and subalpine fir emerge from the dead, gray spruce skeletons. Drought-hardy limber pine and bristlecone pine may increase their range, or not. Drought-hardy mid-elevation lodgepole forests may survive, but continuing pressure by drought, pine beetles, and wildfire is likely to reduce their extent and slowly yield to ponderosa pine, Douglas fir, juniper, and Gambel oak. According to Veblen and the Colorado Natural Heritage Program, aspen and subalpine fir may extend their abundance and range in wetter areas. In turn, the lower-elevation ponderosa pine and Douglas fir forest of the montane are likely to transform to pinyon-juniper woodland, shrubland (e.g., mountain mahogany or sagebrush), or grassland.

Transformation will take a long time, as conifers have large seeds that disperse slowly and prospects for large-scale replanting are not great, due to cost and supply. There will be decades of lag time when vast areas lack any forest, like at the Hayman burn. There are still many hard-to-quantify variables, such as degree of warming, precipitation, insect mortality, and number and extent of wildfires, but ecological change is underway.

Think of the change to our mammal biodiversity since Ouray's time. The buffalo had been exterminated by the late 1800s, grizzly bears and wolves had to be exterminated to protect free-roaming, unregulated livestock grazing on public lands, moose were meat-hunted to extinction, bighorns died out due to disease from domestic sheep and hunting, elk herds were scarce from meat-hunting, lynx and wolverine were trapped out, and beaver nearly so. Vast numbers of sheep and cattle were plugged into those ecological niches, overgrazing the habitat.

Still today, the federal government has a predator control program, killing black bears, mountain lions, coyotes, and wolves (in the northern Rockies), even eagles (*Scientific American* 2012). The federal government kills some 100,000 carnivores every year under the US Department of Agriculture's Wildlife Services program. While the program does more than predator control, killing predators to protect livestock does take up $100 million of the federal budget each year, not to mention the ecological effects of burgeoning elk and deer populations. Since 2000, Wildlife Services operatives have killed at least 2 million native mammals and 15 million native birds. Many of these animals are iconic in the American West and beloved by the public. Several are listed as endangered or threatened under the Endangered Species Act. In 2014, Wildlife Services killed 322 wolves, 61,702 coyotes, 2,930 foxes, 580 black bears, 796 bobcats, 5 golden eagles, and 3 bald eagles. Christopher Ketcham's (2019) "The Rogue Agency" updates this carnage. Ouray would be shocked.

Some of these grievous wildlife losses have been corrected by reintroductions as our public consciousness has evolved. While biologists have been trying to restore our wildlife, their habitat has shrunk because of development and, thanks to climate change, is becoming altered beyond recognition. Other government agencies continue to kill wildlife in service to mostly public land ranchers.

With a reshuffling of habitat, what will happen to our remaining biodiversity: large carnivores, moose, lynx, wolverines (if they return), bighorn sheep, small mammals, mountain bird populations, cutthroat trout, native plants? It is reasonable to assume mobile, adaptable species such as elk, deer, black bears, mountain lions, and wolves could benefit with more areas of suitable habitat, but the others will decline and some species will disappear from their strongholds.

What will happen to our watersheds and snowpack without the forest to trap, shelter, and store snow for delayed runoff and to moisten the landscape? What if there is no snowpack? Water is the source of all life.

There aren't any practical treatments for bark beetles. The warming climate stimulates beetle populations, but we seem to have crossed that bridge decades ago when the spruce and pine beetle outbreaks exploded. Greenhouse gases in the atmosphere aren't going away anytime soon, even if we stopped emitting them. There is some hope that fuel treatments such as thinning and prescribed burns make forests more resilient to beetles, but they are costly and such treatments won't help roadless, wilderness, or high-altitude areas.

What We Must Do

Not all the news is bad. Ecosystems of the future may be different from those we are accustomed to, but life will go on. There is evidence that beetle-killed or burned forests may be good for biodiversity, opening up the canopy for flowers and shrubs that sustain pollinators and other wildlife that form the base of the food chain and a resilient ecosystem.

Climate and forest scientists talk about adaptation to climate change (Rondeau et al. 2017). One component of building resistance is strategies to enhance the ecosystem's capacity to weather a disturbance without loss, or to enhance human community protection. A second component is resilience, meaning strategies to help ecosystems recover from a disturbance after incurring losses, such as restoration with targeted thinning and prescribed fire.

The component of resistance is an opportunity for public land managers to identify geographies where climate change will be less drastic and where native species can persist (refugia) and migrate through (corridors) as they pursue their moving ecological niche of temperature and moisture. Wild Connections' work to identify these areas in Colorado can be of major assistance to public land managers and help ensure that we preserve some of our native species and habitats.

Land managers must be more proactive in forest resilience. Recent emergence of megafires is not limited to Colorado but to the entire western North America and even the entire planet. We need much more prescribed fire and very targeted mitigation or forest fuels reduction (not clear-cuts), especially in the lower-elevation WUI (wildland-urban interface). Ground waste from thinning absent prescribed fire creates an increased fire hazard. Therefore, treatments need to target small, dense trees in the low-elevation WUI. As Susan Prichard (2021) and her many coauthors state, thinning by itself is not a fire reduction strategy nor an ecosystem restoration strategy; it is *logging*. Thinning or fuels reduction won't save houses in the WUI. Thinning followed by prescribed fire is much more effective in reducing wildfire risk in lower-elevation montane forests (Prichard, Peterson, and Jacobson 2010). The lesson to take away is that thinning and fuels reduction cost money. Logging makes money.

In 2022, Congress approved an unprecedented, massive increase in funds to be used primarily for thinning and other forms of logging across about 30 million acres of federal forests over the next decade. Because of the timber lobbyists, these funds allow commercial logging that often targets larger and older trees, which store more carbon and are more resistant to wildfires than younger trees. We need a safety net to protect those trees.

More than 100 scientists with expertise in ecology, forest management, biodiversity, and climate change issued an open letter to US president Joe Biden and members of Congress (US House of Representatives: Document Repository 2021). The scientists urged the leaders to remove provisions promoting logging and fossil fuels from the multitrillion-dollar infrastructure and reconciliation bills. Signed by Tom Veblen and many other eminent scientists, the letter states: "Logging in US forests emits 723 million tons of uncounted CO_2 into our atmosphere each year—more than 10 times the amount emitted by wildfires and tree mortality from insects combined. Greenhouse gas emissions from logging in US forests are now comparable to the annual CO_2 emissions from U.S. coal burning, and annual emissions from the building sector."

Projects like the Ophir Project near Frisco are not going to protect the WUI, restore forest health, and prevent or reduce wildfire. The Forest Service has the mandate to cut forests and provide jobs in the woods, but these timber sales shouldn't be disguised as thinning to reduce wildfire threat and, since they contribute to climate change, should be scrutinized more thoroughly. Regarding prescribed fire, budgets are slim and managers are risk averse especially for prescribed fire near the WUI. There have indeed been spectacular failures in executing prescribed fires, but the longer we put it off, the worse the fires will be. We must let fires burn in wilderness and roadless areas, even if they scar our trails. But the take-home message from researchers is that climate is the greatest driver of wildfire, and forest management, especially thinning, is unlikely to reduce wildfire hazards.

We may have lost millions of acres of forest, but there are millions remaining, and some lost forest will probably regenerate in some fashion. Our forests and our planet deserve our best efforts to slow or stop warming, to improve forest management, and to promote resilience in our forest ecosystems. Tania Schoennagel (2017) from CU has led a team of experts to advise land managers on how to best build resilience to wildfires, especially in the WUI. Most of these lands are private and it is a complex societal problem to foster change. Pritchard says that, increasingly, managed wildfires ("let it burn") can be suppressed in some areas and let burn in others based on forest conditions. Such a strategy can lead to greater forest resilience.

Human communities must also be more resilient. As Boone Kauffman (2004) said nearly twenty years ago, increasing wildfire is a land use issue; those houses in the WUI must be of fire-resistant construction or not located in the WUI at all. There is a National Wildland Fire Cohesive Strategy formed by the Departments of Agriculture (Forest Service) and Interior (BLM, NPS) that stresses a multipronged approach, and the Colorado State Forest Service has a recent Forest Action Plan. While good first steps, these plans skirt the kind of political change needed for forest health and human habitation in the wildfire zone. We need to change land use, building codes, and insurance practices to discourage building new homes and to "harden" existing homes in the WUI.

Roughly half of Colorado's population lives in the WUI, and a third nationwide. The recent Marshall Fire is redefining the term WUI to include towns and cities near grasslands. In fact, all of Colorado is vulnerable because once a grass fire reaches a town, the town becomes an urban fire, consuming even newer construction. Like the lessons of the 1800–early 1900s that prompted house and buildings made of brick and stone, our homes and buildings are not made to resist high winds and flying embers. We have been confident that our fire departments and water systems could protect our cities, but the Marshall Fire thoroughly debunked that theory.

The CT travels above the WUI except at certain roads and trailheads. Although one rarely sees homes from the trail, the fire burns uphill and fires started in the WUI could burn through the trail corridor. I myself have lived in the forested WUI, and I did not remove all the pines near my house. I understand homeowners' reluctance to do so. But one has to realize living there is a calculated risk, a risk you could lose it all. My own risk tolerance has changed with the megafires of 2020–2021.

There is a belief among many scientists that we cannot affect the total area burned by fire, as this is driven strongly by climate. Wildfire is big business in the United States; some call it the fire-industrial complex. Since 2002, the cost of federal wildfire protection and suppression has averaged more than $3 billion per year, accounting for nearly half of the Forest Service's annual budget. While it is human nature to expect government to protect homes and towns, we need to lower the expectation that the government and taxpayers can be relied on to save lives and protect those homes in the WUI, especially those who do not make their homes fire resistant. The towns of Superior and Louisville are considering requiring tougher building codes to make new construction more fireproof; maybe all of Colorado should follow.

Besides fire-proofing their homes, WUI residents need to form and finance their own fire protection districts, where none exist, and to do community wildland fire protection plans and mitigation as well as fight fire. Of course, this will take funding, nearly all of which comes in the form of some kind of taxes that many Americans oppose. If we had some type of carbon tax, it would not only reduce greenhouse gases and the effects of climate change;

it could also help fund the transition to renewable energy and be a big boost toward funding and managing our forests and mitigating fire in the WUI.

About 84 percent of wildfire ignitions and 44 percent of area burned are from human ignitions, including campfires, powerlines, fireworks, hunting, vehicles, and other equipment use. In 2020, an unattended campfire ignited the Ice Lakes Fire, at one of the most beautiful areas in the San Juans. I think the CTF should promote a fire ban along the entire trail. Most backpackers observe LNT and use stoves anyway.

Most important for the long run, there is urgent need to aggressively tax carbon and substantially reduce our society's carbon emissions. Not just for our forests but for our entire way of life. While only our government can lead the real change, we each can make decisions to reduce our criminal carbon footprint, which far exceeds the rest of the world's citizens. There are great carbon footprint calculators online. Try one or two like I did, and have your eyes opened to where your carbon pollution is greatest (e.g., air travel, your car, and beef). The State of Colorado's Greenhouse Gas Reduction Roadmap (2021) has taken a modest step forward with goals of reducing greenhouse gas emissions by at least 26 percent by 2025, by at least 50 percent by 2030, and by at least 90 percent by 2050. More is needed.

The Bureau of Land Management continues to offer up massive tracts of public lands for oil and gas leasing despite the fact that United States Geological Survey (USGS) has determined that a fourth of all America's greenhouse gases originate from public lands; 12 percent of that comes from Colorado (Merrill 2018). Recently, President Biden approved the Willow Project in Alaska, an oil and gas "carbon bomb" on public lands. Drilling and leasing on public lands are ongoing and need to stop. This activity violates Colorado's Greenhouse Roadmap and our agreements to the Paris and Glasgow Climate Conferences. Tell your land managers and legislators we must stop criminal fossil fuel leasing and development on our public lands in favor of renewable energy.

At the close of 2021, 770,000 Covid deaths had been reported. The Marshall Fire spread destruction in the towns of Superior and Louisville. A mere week later, spurred by a corrupt former president, insurrectionists attacked our capitol while Congress was in session and threatened to kill or injure our elected representatives. But for a valiant fight by Capitol Police, they might have succeeded in overthrowing the government. In the ensuing political debate, climate change was put on the back burner again.

Who is to blame for this national climate threat? It's easy to blame the oil and coal industries, since they aggressively lobby for candidates, subsidies, and protections, but it's really everyone who uses fossil fuels—all of us. In 1970, the Earth Day Pogo comic strip once said, "We have met the enemy and he is us!" We desperately need a new national paradigm that replaces fossil fuels with renewable energy.

I Hope

After the 2020 election, I was hopeful that our government would take decisive intervention on our use of fossil fuels and make a wholescale conversion to renewable energy. President Biden attempted to insert climate change into his Build Back Better bill, but Senate Democrats Joe Manchin and Kyrsten Sinema opposed it, and by just those two votes it failed to pass. Manchin is from West Virginia and caters to the coal and fossil fuel vote. I have to call out these two "Democrats" (and the bloc-voting Republicans) because they will have to live with the legacy of that vote and the grave consequences for history. We had a rare chance to act, and they undermined their own party to oppose it. It may be too late for some of our forests and will take time and vast investment, but there is much we can save.

Despite a politically divided country, when the fires, hurricanes, and floods got severe enough, Congress finally took action. As part of the 2022 Inflation Reduction Act, the REPLANT Act will help reforest 4.1 million acres by planting 1.2 billion trees over the next ten years. Planting these trees will sequester 75 million metric tons of carbon in a decade, which is equivalent to avoiding the use of 8.5 billion gal. of gasoline. There are other climate provisions of the bill that are a major step forward in meeting the Paris Accords.

Hope for a better life is the essence of humanity. If we could all just agree on what base principles we hope for, maybe we could all reach a greater harmony. My greatest hope is that we as a people decide that the planet's health is key to our health, security, and well-being.

At the ground level, I am pleased that the vast Hermosa area has received wilderness-level protection with the 2014 legislation passed during the Obama Administration with the guidance of Colorado senator Michael Bennet. I am so pleased that President Biden designated the Camp Hale–Continental Divide National Monument. We need to vigilantly protect our wild areas from development to protect biodiversity and, yes, outdoor recreation. The 30×30 Initiative is a national campaign to protect 30 percent of lands, rivers, lakes, and wetlands by 2030. Of course, this will help. Especially, we need to identify and protect wildlife refugia and corridors in our wild areas. Corridors require habitat that is connected across vast distances, where a wider ecosystem of flora and wildlife can flourish. Since so much habitat has been developed or fragmented, these pathways are rare and becoming rarer.

I can report the CT is much more popular than it was fifteen years ago. We met or passed five to twenty people a day, many of them mountain bike riders. Along the Monarch Crest, we were passed by more than 100 riders in one day. The trail is clean, and campsites I saw were in good shape. Invasive species were minimal, except a few that are found everywhere, like the common mullein that I observed at lower elevations where cattle graze. I was pleased to find Leave No Trace conditions on the CT were very good with regard to those principles. The Colorado Trail Foundation is constantly maintaining the tread of the trail; it is well signed and easy to follow.

In chapter 1, I cited the CTF's vision to provide a unique, "high-altitude experience to support environmental education, an avenue for healing and self-renewal, an appreciation for the value of natural systems, to encourage a cooperative effort to maintain these systems, and to promote a sense of public ownership."

I interviewed Steve Staley, chairman of the board of the Colorado Trail Foundation, about the science of forest health and climate change and the CT. Steve indicated the CTF avoids any advocacy or policy positions related to social, political, or environmental matters, deferring those decisions to the land managers. Hence, they do not speak out on issues like proposed wildernesses or climate change. He indicated they do comment on forest plans and coordinate with the CDT National Scenic Trail corridor.

I asked whether the CTF would support educational or citizen science projects aimed at educating hikers and providing data to land managers on forest health. While the CTF mission embraces education, and its vision seeks "appreciation for the value of natural systems, and encourages a cooperative effort to maintain these systems" (Colorado Trail Foundation n.d.), Mr. Staley indicated CTF is only concerned with building and maintaining a quality trail and doesn't perform such programs as they are "outside its scope of operations." I find this inconsistent with the CTF mission and vision. It is understandable that they want to take the tried-and-true path, so to speak, of focusing only on the tread and keeping their collective head down on "political or environmental matters." They don't want trouble with donors, the Forest Service, or local politicians. But they are well established and really have little to lose and the intangible leadership mantle to gain.

In contrast, all three long trails—the AT, CDT and PCT—are actively educating about climate change. The AT employs seasonal "ridgerunners" to educate hikers about LNT and to do light maintenance. The Forest Service recognizes climate change and is actively analyzing adaptation strategies. Mr. Staley is a gentleman; he read and complimented the manuscript, patiently listened to me, and is devoted to the CTF. I respect him even though I disagree with him. But urgent times call for leaders to step up and make their voice heard. I hope CTF will do so someday.

Finally, I asked whether the CTF would consider using their platforms to encourage hikers to reduce their personal carbon footprints by car or air travel by purchasing greenhouse gas emission offsets from reputable organizations such as Terrapass. Terrapass carbon offsets fund projects like reforestation, farm power, and landfill gas capture to remove carbon from the environment: https://terrapass.com/. Mr. Staley said only if there was an easy way to do so.

I wonder if in his elder years, Ouray still had hope that his people would ever have their homelands, to practice their way of life unmolested by Americans hell-bent on their conquest of the Utes and the landscape. I believe he and Chipeta reflected with sadness and hope for the future of their people. A scant 140 years and 6 million people later, Colorado today would be beyond his wildest imagining. I too reflect with sadness on a global threat but hold hope for us all. And for wild nature as we know it.

After several doctor visits, Frosty was diagnosed with giardia, the bane of backpackers. Despite treating all of his water, the bug got to him. Initially, he tested negative. When he didn't get better, his doctor put him on Flagyl. With medication, it cleared right up. Brian the Bishop returned home and is fine. He completed his sabbatical and is back at work. I think both guys would like to finish the trail sometime. Grasshopper and I will probably hike again someday, as long as our bodies let us.

I was pleased that I can still hike the still-majestic mountains and that my body held up well during the hike. I know I was much fitter after the hike, but I wondered if the nature fix had measurably impacted my health. Recall that blood pressure, along with stress hormones, can be adversely affected by our American lifestyle. I had my annual physical after I returned and I had lost 5 lb., my blood pressure was down 25 points, and my hematocrit was up 7 points!

The Colorado Trail is the signature trail in the state and one of the best long trails in the country. It will endure as long as hikers seek refuge and solace from our complicated lives, as long as good people like the Colorado Trail Foundation and its volunteers and donors are willing to maintain it, and as long as we remain vigilant in protecting our public lands. The ecology of the trail will change in the coming decades, but it will still offer beauty and solace to its pilgrims.

I hope the forests and the trail will be there for my grandchildren and that they can find beauty, peace, and renewal like I did. I also hope they appreciate the beauty of the complexity of our ecosystems that sustain us. And that we acted in time to save most of our forests and wildlife. I hope to be back again.

Acknowledgments

I owe a big debt to Dr. Tom Veblen, Distinguished Professor Emeritus of Geography, University of Colorado, for consenting to an interview with me and actually reviewing the manuscript to correct and clarify my errors in the science of forest health in Colorado. Anonymous reviewers provided additional scientific insights and suggestions. Thanks to Steve Staley, chairman of the board, Colorado Trail Foundation, for reading the manuscript, consenting to an interview, and patiently listening to me when he could have just blown me off. Thanks to Nate Bauer of the University Press of Colorado for leading me through the process of my first published book, and to the expert help of Laura Furney, also of UPC. Thanks also to Sonya Manes for her editing skills and making the text better. Thanks to Sarah Gorecki, Colorado Mountain Club Press, for reviewing the early manuscript and providing excellent comments. I only wished I could get CMC Press to publish this book, but they are backed up with other projects in the queue and she generously gave of her time and expertise. Thanks to Jonathon Stewart, accomplished long-distance hiker, public lands advocate, and author, for your support. Thanks to Frosty for his companionship and review of an early manuscript and to Grasshopper and Carla for their hiking companionship. Thanks to the board members of Wild Connections (wildconnections.org) for giving me a platform to voice forest health and climate change issues and for mapping climate corridors in the eastern half of the Colorado Trail. Thanks to giants of conservation mentors like Aldo Leopold, John Muir, and Ed Abbey, whom I was lucky to meet. Thanks to John Fielder, who inspired me to hike the wilderness and Gudy Gaskill, who was the force behind the Colorado Trail. I am thankful to my parents, who introduced me to nature, and to my family, who shared that life with me. Finally, thanks to Anne Ford for supporting us on our hike and my writing of this book, and for being my wonderful partner.

Appendix A

Leave only (Small) Footprints

Reprinted from *Landscapes* 2019.

Leave no trace policy teaches us to take only photographs and leave only footprints. In our publications, we emphasize traveling lightly on the environment and restoring damaged ecosystems. But speaking of footprints, have you heard about carbon footprints and do you know what your carbon footprint is? In this article, I use greenhouse gases (GHG) and carbon interchangeably.

Before tackling that question, it is good to remind ourselves that climate change is caused by atmospheric, human-caused GHG and poses an existential threat to our lifestyle as well as our planetary ecosystems. In your lifetime or your children's lifetime, it will be time to pay the piper. The choices we make today (and all those yesterdays) will determine the legacy we leave to future generations. At this stage in my life, I think about that legacy a lot. Stabilizing world population will help, but we must change lifestyle too. Whether we will have enough water, enough food, our wild places and species, whether we will be inundated with climate refugees from our own or other countries and whether we have food and water security. These are already major problems around the world, and we are not isolated by the oceans.

Regardless of what our politicians do or don't do about the carbon load on our planet, we can choose to be responsible for our own personal lifestyle choices and our contribution to the GHG load. The average American lifestyle is among the highest in the world, emitting 15–30 *tons* of carbon dioxide equivalent (methane and other gases contribute) per person! For comparison, your car weighs around 2 tons. Many other countries' per capita emissions are much, much less, from 5.6 *tons* in the UK to even less than 1 ton. I'm not saying you must forego children, live in a tipi, and give up your car, but there may be much you can do. According to the IPCC, we need to reduce the carbon equivalents by half to meet the Paris Agreement (2023).

There are multiple carbon footprint (CF) estimators out there including ones by EPA and The Nature Conservancy. (I have noticed inconsistencies in various estimates due to assumptions.) I like the latter because it is more complete. There are about five major sectors: personal transportation (your car), air travel, home heating and electrical, food, and consumption of goods and services. I have an efficient automobile; I carpool and combine trips and try to keep my mileage down to 8,000 miles/year (below average). I'm reducing my airplane trips because I indulged last year (no one is perfect, right?). I have solar electricity for my house and our house is small and energy-efficient. I recycle. Finally, I am becoming more of a vegetarian, although not strict vegetarian. Meat, especially beef, is outrageously high in carbon emissions to produce.

In fact, livestock production (especially beef) contributes more than 14 percent of global GHG emissions, about equal to the transportation or home heating or electricity! (Note, in the US, figures differ and transportation emits about 29% due to our "affluence.") With my changes, my CF is around 12 tons and I hope to still reduce it further. I am planning energy conservation measures to my house and have an electric vehicle.

What is Wild Connections doing to advocate for a lower CF? Of course, we carpool to meetings, hikes, and projects, and may do tree planting projects. But specifically, we adopted a policy of supporting reductions of fossil fuel production GHG on public lands to meet the Colorado Climate Plan, which is a 26 percent reduction in GHG by 2020, a 50 percent reduction by 2030 and a 90 percent reduction by 2050.

If Americans can cut their CF by half, we could meet the Colorado Climate Plan, the Paris Agreement goals, and help ensure a healthy legacy to future generations (https://www.nature.com/articles/d41586-018-06876-2).

And finally, we must have political leadership to do their part to help us get there. **Vote**!

Appendix B

Letter to Editor, *Denver Post*

Submitted March 20, 2022.

LTE apologists for Big Oil and Georgia politicians against the electric truck manufacturer Rivian (March 20) are standing for a planetary crisis that will make the war in Ukraine small potatoes. No disrespect to the brave Ukrainians. Climate change poses a war of attrition that has taken a hundred years to arrive and will last for thousands of years.

Coloradans feel safe from sea level rise, hurricanes, millions, if not billions of climate refugees and global tumult as water and food shortages begin displacing refugees on a scale never imagined. Here at home, wildfires and drought are eating away our forests and snowpack and burning our cities. Over 1 million Coloradans reside in the highly vulnerable 'wildland urban interface,' and that definition did not include Louisville/Superior. Until now.

There are many scientific papers documenting the loss of our mountain forests to drought, beetles and wildfire and, it is likely most of these lands may never regrow forest at all. There are papers projecting the complete loss of our mountain snowpack by 2062 and alarming loss and timing of streamflow, so critical to our cities and farms. These impacts are largely and ultimately tied to our use of fossil fuels, and greenhouse gas contribution grows daily.

President Biden and Governor Polis have advocated for renewable energy and electric vehicles as a partial solution, but we need to do so much more to win the war and protect our homeland. What kind of world do you stand for?

References

(with Some Annotations)

Abatzoglou, John T., and A. Park Williams. 2016. "Impact of Anthropogenic Climate Change on Wildfire across Western US Forests." *PNAS* 113 (42): 11770–11775. https://doi.org/10.1073/pnas.1607171113.

Adams, Rick A., and Mark A. Hayes. 2018. "Assemblage-level Analysis of Sex-Ratios in Coloradan Bats in Relation to Climate Variables: A Model for Future Expectations." *Global Ecology and Conservation* 14 (April). https://doi.org/10.1016/j.gecco.2018.e00379.

Andrus, R. A., R. K. Chai, B. J. Harvey, K. C. Rodman, and T. T. Veblen. 2021. "Increasing Rates of Subalpine Tree Mortality Linked to Warmer and Drier Summers." *Journal of Ecology* 109:2203–2218.

Andrus, Robert A., Sarah J. Hart, and Thomas T. Veblen. 2020. "Forest Recovery following Synchronous Outbreaks of Spruce and Western Balsam Bark Beetle Is Slowed by Ungulate Browsing." *Ecology* 101 (5). https://doi.org/10.1002/ecy.2998.

Andrus, Robert A., Sarah J. Hart, Niko Tutland, Thomas T. Veblen. 2021. "Future Dominance by Quaking Aspen Expected following Short-Interval, Compounded Disturbance Interaction." *Ecosphere* 12 (1). https://doi.org/10.1002/ecs2.3345.

Athearn, Frederick. 1977. *An Isolated Empire: A History of Northwest Colorado.* BLM Cultural Resource Series, Colorado No. 12. https://archive.org/details

/isolatedempirehiooathe_1. (This is a great summary of the Ute Tribe's encounters with white Americans.)

Battaglia, Mike A., Benjamin Gannon, Peter M. Brown, Paula J. Fornwalt, Antony S. Cheng, and Laurie Kay Stroh Huckaby. 2018. "Changes in Forest Structure since 1860 in Ponderosa Pine Dominated Forests in the Colorado and Wyoming Front Range, USA." *Forest Ecology and Management* 422:147–160.

Benedict, Audrey. 2008. *The Naturalist's Guide to the Southern Rockies, Colorado, Southern Wyoming and Northern New Mexico*. Golden, CO: Wheat Ridge Fulcrum Publishing.

Blair, Rob. 1996. *The Western San Juan Mountains: Their Geology, Ecology and Human History*. Boulder: University Press of Colorado.

Bowler, Diana. 2021. "Complex Causes of Insect Declines." *Nature, Ecology and Evolution* 5:1334–1335. (For the Uncompahgre Fritillary, see the US Fish and Wildlife Service site, https://www.fws.gov/species/uncompahgre-fritillary-butterfly-boloria-acrocnema.)

Bureau of Land Management. n.d. *BLM Rangeland Health Status* (Map).

Chambers, Marin, Colorado Forest Restoration Institute, and Colorado State University. 2020. "As Wildfires Become More Intense, Forests May Not Grow Back." *National Public Radio, Environment and Energy Collaborative*, September 13. (Also, the video is outstanding: see Julie Speer Jackson, "Colorado Experience: Forests of Change," Rocky Mountain Public Broadcasting Service, 2020, Denver.)

Chiodi, Andrew M., Brian E. Potter, and Narasimhan K. Larkin. 2021. "Multidecadal Change in Western US Nighttime Vapor Pressure Deficit." *Geophysical Research Letters*. https://doi.org/10.1029/2021GL092830.

Colorado Climate Center. n.d. "Drought History." https://climate.colostate.edu/drought_info.html. (And for US Drought Monitor history, see https://www.drought.gov/states/colorado#historical-conditions.)

Colorado Natural Heritage Program. 2020. *Guide to Ecological Systems of Colorado*. Fort Collins: Colorado State University. https://cnhp.colostate.edu/download/documents/EcolSystems/EcologicalSystemsofColorado2020.pdf.

Colorado Parks and Wildlife. 2014. "Lynx in Colorado." Denver. https://cpw.state.co.us/conservation/Pages/CON-Lynx.aspx. (For wolverines, see "Wolverine," https://cpw.state.co.us/learn/Pages/Wolverine.aspx.)

Colorado Parks and Wildlife. 2023a. *Final Wolf Restoration and Management Plan*. Denver. https://cpw.state.co.us/learn/Pages/CON-Wolf-Management.aspx.

Colorado Parks and Wildlife. 2023b. *Rocky Mountain Elk*. https://cpw.state.co.us/conservation/Pages/CON-Elk.aspx.

Colorado Parks and Wildlife. Wetland Wildlife Conservation Program. n.d. https://cpw.state.co.us/aboutus/Pages/Wetlands.aspx.

Colorado Public Radio. 2021. "After 20 Years of Drought, Western Slope Ranchers Face a Choice—Keep Adapting, or Move Along." July 23. https://www.cpr.org/2021/07/23/western-slope-drought-cattle-ranching/.

Colorado State Forest Service. 2020. *2020 Report on the Health of Colorado's Forests.* Fort Collins: Colorado State University.

Colorado Trail Foundation. 2008. *The Colorado Trail/.* Denver: Colorado Mountain Club Press. 7th ed. (The 2017 9th ed. is the most current version.)

Colorado Trail Foundation. 2018. *The Colorado Trail Databook.* 7th ed. Denver: Colorado Mountain Club Press.

Colorado Trail Foundation website. n.d. https://coloradotrail.org/colorado-trail-foundation/.

Coop, Jonathan D., et al. 2020. "Wildfire-Driven Forest Conversion in Western North American Landscapes." *BioScience* 70 (8): 659–673. https://doi.org/10.1093/biosci/biaa061.

Cox, Mark. 2021. Interview with Tom Bellinger, MSU Denver. https://red.msudenver.edu/2021/the-case-of-the-disappearing-glaciers/#:~:text=The%20largest%20(and%20maybe%20craggiest,century%20and%20continues%20to%20decline.

Davis, Kimberley T., Marcos D. Robles, Kerry B. Kemp, et al. (62 total authors). 2023. "Reduced Fire Severity Offers Near-Term Buffer to Climate-Driven Declines in Conifer Resilience across the Western United States." *PNAS* 120 (11). https://doi.org/10.1073/pnas.2208120120.

Demographic Statistics. 2023. "Historical Census Population of Colorado 1870–2000." Accessed October 17. https://dtdapps.coloradodot.info/staticdata/Statistics/dsp_folder/Demographic/HistoricalCensus.htm.

Domke, Grant M., and others. 2020. "Greenhouse Gas Emissions and Removals from Forest Land, Woodlands, and Urban Trees in the United States, 1990–2018." *Resource Update FS-227.* Madison, WI: Department of Agriculture, Forest Service, Northern Research Station. e0263779. https://www.fs.usda.gov/research/treesearch/62418.

Fielder, John, and John Fayhee. 1992. *Along the Colorado Trail.* Englewood, CO: Westcliffe Publishers.

Fielder, John, and Mark Pearson. 2002. *The Complete Guide to Colorado's Wilderness Areas.* Englewood, CO: Westcliffe Publishing.

Finley, Bruce. 2016. "Colorado Embarks on Experimental 'Predator Control' Killing of More Lions and Bears to Try to Save Dwindling Deer." *Denver Post,* December 13, 2016.

Ford, Karl. 2021. *Triple Crown Hiking Adventures: 8,000 miles on America's Long Trails.* Kindle books.

Formica, Adam, Emily C. Farrer, and Isabel W. Ashton. 2014. "Shrub Expansion over the Past 62 Years in Rocky Mountain Alpine Tundra: Possible Causes and Consequences." *Arctic and Alpine Research.* 46 (3): 616–631. https://doi.org/10.1657/1938-4246-46.3.616.

Funk, Jason, Steven Saunders, Brian F. Walters, David J. Nowak, James Smith, Stephen M. Ogle, J. W. Coulston, and T. C. Wirth. 2014. "Rocky Mountain Forests at Risk: Confronting Climate-Driven Impacts from Insects, Wildfires, Heat, and Drought. Union of Concerned Scientists and Rocky Mountain Climate Organization." Cambridge.

Gerber, P. J., H. Steinfeld, B. Henderson, A. Mottet, C. Opio, J. Dijkman, A. Falcucci, and G. Tempio. 2013. *Tackling Climate Change through Livestock: A Global Assessment of Emissions and Mitigation Opportunities*. Rome: Food and Agriculture Organization of the United Nations (FAO).

Graham, Russell T., technical ed. 2003. "Hayman Fire Case Study." *General Technical Reports RMRS-GTR-114*. Ogden, UT: Department of Agriculture, Forest Service, Rocky Mountain Research Station. 396 pp.

Gulliford, Andrew. 2021. *The Woolly West: Colorado's Hidden History of Sheepscapes*. Lubbock: Texas A&M University Press.

Hardin, Garrett. 1968. "The Tragedy of the Commons." 1968. *Science* 162, no. 3859 (December 13): 1243–1248. https://doi.org/10.1126/science.162.3859.1243.

Hayhoe, Katherine. 2021. *Saving Us: A Climate Scientist's Case for Hope and Healing in a Divided World*. New York: One Signal Publishers.

Hood, Grace. n.d. "Soldierstone." KUNC. http://hiddencolorado.kunc.org/soldierstone/.

Iglesias, Virginia, Jennifer Balch, and William Travis. 2022. "U.S. Fires Became Larger, More Frequent, and More Widespread in the 2000s." *Science Advances* 8, no. 11 (March 16). https://doi.org/10.1126/sciadv.abc0020.

Inouye, David. 2020. "Effects of Climate Change on Alpine Plants and Their Pollinators." *Annals of the New York Academy of Sciences* 1469, no. 1 (June): 26–37.

Inouye, David, Billy Barr, Kenneth B. Armitage, and Brian D. Inouye. 2000. "Climate Change Is Affecting Altitudinal Migrants and Hibernating Species." *PNAS* 97 (4): 1630–1633. https://doi.org/10.1073/pnas.97.4.1630.

Intergovernmental Panel on Climate Change. 2023. *Climate Change 2022: Mitigation of Climate Change. Contribution of Working Group III to the Sixth Assessment Report of the Intergovernmental Panel on Climate Change*, edited by P. R. Shukla, J. Skea, R. Slade, A. Al Khourdajie, R. van Diemen, D. McCollum, M. Pathak, S. Some, P. Vyas, R. Fradera, M. Belkacemi, A. Hasija, G. Lisboa, and S. Luz, J. Malley. New York: Cambridge University Press.

Janousek, William M., Margaret R. Douglas, and Syd Cannings. 2023. "Recent and Future Declines of a Historically Widespread Pollinator Linked to Climate, Land Cover, and Pesticides." *PNAS* 120 (5): e2211223120. https://doi.org/10.1073/pnas.2211223120.

Kauffman, J. Boone. 2004. "Death Rides the Forest: Perceptions of Fire, Land Use and Ecological Restoration of Western Forests." *Conservation Biology* 18, no. 4 (July 23) https://doi.org/10.1111/j.1523-1739.2004.545_1.x.

Ketcham, Christopher. 2018. "The Rogue Agency." New York. *Harper's Magazine*. https://harpers.org/archive/2016/03/the-rogue-agency/.

Knowles, John F., Peter D. Blanken, Corey R. Lawrence, and Mark W. Williams. 2019. "Evidence for Non-Steady-State Carbon Emissions from Snow-Scoured Alpine Tundra." *Nature Communications* 10 (1306). https://doi.org/10.1038/s41467-019-09149-2.

Kolbert, Elizabeth. *The Sixth Extinction: An Unnatural History.* 2014. New York: Henry Holt and Company. (A comprehensive account of how humans are causing the latest and greatest human extinction crisis in our planet's history.)

Leave No Trace Principles. n.d. https://lnt.org/why/7-principles/.

Leopold, Aldo. 1966. *A Sand County Almanac.* New York: Ballantine Books.

Lukas, Jeff, lead author, and Joseph Barsugli, Nolan Doesken, Imtiaz Rangwala, and Klaus Wolter. 2014. *Climate Change in Colorado: A Synthesis to Support Water Resources Management and Adaptation.* A Report for the Colorado Water Conservation Board Western Water Assessment, Cooperative Institute for Research in Sciences (CIRES), University of Colorado Boulder.

Mattson, Dave, and Troy Merrill, 2021. "Modeling Restoration Areas for Grizzly Bears in the Southwest." Report. *Grizzly Bear Recovery Project Technical Paper* GBRP-TP-2021-3/.

McCain, Christy M., Sarah R. B. King, and Tim M. Szewczyk. 2021. "Unusually Large Upward Shifts in Cold-Adapted, Montane Mammals as Temperature Warms." *Ecology* 102 (4). https://doi.org/10.1002/ecy.3300.

Meaney, C. A., and D. Van Vuren. 1993. "Recent Distribution of Bison in Colorado West of the Great Plains." *Proceedings of the Denver Museum of Natural History* 3:1–10.

Merrill, Matthew D., Benjamin M. Sleeter, Phillip A. Freeman, Jinxun Liu, Peter D. Warwick, and Bradley C. Reed. 2018. *Federal Lands Greenhouse Gas Emissions and Sequestration in the United States: Estimates for 2005–14.* Geological Survey Scientific Investigations Report 2018-5131.

Millennium Ecosystem Reports. n.d. https://www.millenniumassessment.org/en/Index-2.html.

Milly, P. C. D., and K. A. Dunne. 2020. "Colorado River Flow Dwindles as Warming-Driven Loss of Reflective Snow Energizes Evaporation." *Science* 367 (6483). https://doi.org/10.1126/science.aay9187.

Mountain Studies Institute. 2012. *Climate Change Assessment for the San Juan Mountain Regions, Southwestern Colorado, USA: A Review of Scientific Research.* Silverton, CO: Prepared in Cooperation with USDA Forest Service San Juan National Forest and USDOI Bureau of Land Management.

Mueller, Andy. n.d. "Rising Temperatures and Declining Flows: The Current and Likely Future of the Colorado River Basin." https://roaringfork.org/media/2196/20201015-andy-mueller-presenation-for-brooksher-watershed-institute.pdf.

Muir, John. 1902. *Our National Parks.* Boston, New York: Houghton Mifflin and Company.

National Audubon Society. 2023. "How Climate Change Will Reshape the Range of the Brown-capped Rosy-Finch." https://www.audubon.org/field-guide/bird/brown-capped-rosy-finch?adm1=CO&country=US#bird-climate-vulnerability.

National Geographic Society Resource Library. 2023. "Megafire." https://www.nationalgeographic.org/encyclopedia/megafire/.

National Interagency Fire Center. n.d. "Wildfire Statistics." https://www.nifc.gov/fire-information/statistics.

National Park Service. n.d. Mission. https://www.nps.gov/aboutus/aboutus.htm#:~:text=The%20mission%20of%20the%20National,of%20this%20and%20future%20generations.

National Wilderness Preservation System. n.d. "National Wilderness Preservation System." https://en.wikipedia.org/wiki/National_Wilderness_Preservation_System.

Nelson, Richard. *The Island Within*. 1989. San Francisco: North Point Press. (A beautifully written book about man and nature in offshore islands in British Columbia.)

Petersen, David. 1998. *Ghost Grizzlies: Does the Great Bear Still Haunt Colorado?* Chicago: Johnson Books.

Prichard, Susan, and 19 others. 2021. "Adapting Western North American Forests to Climate Change and Wildfires: 10 Common Questions." *Ecological Applications* 31 (8): 2021, e02433. https://doi.org/10.1002/eap.2433.

Prichard, Susan, David L. Peterson, and Kyle Jacobson. 2010. "Fuel Treatments Reduce the Severity of Wildfire Effects in Dry Mixed Conifer Forest. Washington, USA." *Canadian Journal of Forest Research* 40 (8). https://doi.org/10.1139/X10-109.

Public Lands Foundation. 2014. "Public Lands, Origin, History, Future." https://publicland.org/wp-content/uploads/2016/08/150359_Public_Lands_Document_web.pdf.

Quresh, Latif, Jacob Ivan, Amy Seglund, David Pavlacky, and Richard Truex. 2020. "Avian Relationships with Bark Beetle Outbreaks and Underlying Mechanisms in Lodgepole Pine and Spruce-Fir Forests of Colorado." *Forest Ecology and Management* 464. https://doi.org/10.1016/j.foreco.2020.118043.

Reid, Colleen E., Emma S. Rieves, and Kate Carlson. 2022. "Perceptions of Green Space Usage, Abundance, and Quality of Green Space Were Associated with Better Mental Health during the COVID-19 Pandemic among Residents of Denver." *Plos One* 7 (3). https://journals.plos.org/plosone/article?id=10.1371/journal.pone.0263779.

Reyher, Ken. 2002. *High Country Cowboys: A History of Ranching in Western Colorado*. Lake City, CO: Western Reflections Publishing Company.

Rice, Janine R., Linda A. Joyce, Claudia Regan, David Winters, and Rick Truex. 2020. "Climate Change Vulnerability Assessment of Aquatic and Terrestrial Ecosystems in the U.S. Forest Service Rocky Mountain Region." *General Technical*

Reports RMRS-GTR-376. 216 pp. Fort Collins, CO: Department of Agriculture, Forest Service, Rocky Mountain Research Station.

Rick, Brianna. 2022. "The Real Glaciers of Colorado." Fort Collins: Colorado State University. https://sustainability.colostate.edu/humannature/the-real-glaciers-of-colorado/.

Rockström, J., W. Steffen, K. Noone, and Å. Persson, et al. 2009. "Planetary Boundaries: Exploring the Safe Operating Space for Humanity." *Nature* 461:472–475. https://doi.org/10.1038/461472a. (Appears online as "A Safe Operating Space for Humanity.")

Rocky Mountain Restoration Initiative San Juan Mountains Project Fact Sheet. n.d. https://restoringtherockies.org/wp-content/uploads/2020/09/7351a-southwest-project-information-sheet-updated.pdf.

Rodman, Kyle C., Robert A. Andrus, Amanda R. Carlson, Trevor A. Carter, Teresa B. Chapman, Jonathan D. Coop, Paula J. Fornwalt, Nathan S. Gill, Brian J. Harvey, Ashley E. Hoffman, Katharine C. Kelsey, Dominik Kulakowski, Daniel C. Laughlin, Jenna E. Morris, José F. Negrón, Katherine M. Nigro, Gregory S. Pappas, Miranda D. Redmond, Charles C. Rhoades, Monique E. Rocca, Zoe H. Schapira, Jason S. Sibold, Camille S. Stevens-Rumann, Thomas T. Veblen, Jianmin Wang, Xiaoyang Zhang, and Sarah J. Hart. 2022. "Rocky Mountain Forests Are Poised to Recover following Bark Beetle Outbreaks but with Altered Composition." *Journal of Ecology*. https://doi.org/10.1111/1365-2745.13999.

Rodman, Kyle C., Thomas T. Veblen, Mike A. Battaglia, Marin E. Chambers, Paula J. Fornwalt, Zachary A. Holden, Thomas E. Kolb, Jessica R. Ouzts, and Monica T. Rother. 2020. "A Changing Climate Is Snuffing Out Post-fire Recovery in Montane Forests." *Global Ecology and Biogeography* 29 (11): 2039–2051.

Romero, Jonathan. 2016. *Durango Herald*, February 17.

Rondeau, R., B. Neely, M. Bidwell, I. Rangwala, L. Yung, K. Clifford, and T. Schulz. 2017. "Spruce-Fir Landscape: Upper Gunnison River Basin, Colorado. Social-Ecological Climate Resilience Project." Agency report. North Central Climate Science Center, Fort Collins, Colorado.

Rosenberg, Kenneth, et al. 2019. "Decline of the North American Avifauna." *Science* 19 366, no. 6461 (September): 120–124. https://doi.org/10.1126/science.aaw1313.

Rusho, W. L. 1983. *Everett Ruess: A Vagabond for Beauty*. Layton, UT: Gibbs M. Smith Publishing.

Scharnagl, Klara, David Johnson, and Diane Ebert-May. 2019. "Shrub Expansion and Alpine Plant Community Change: 40-Year Record from Niwot Ridge, Colorado." *Plant Ecology and Diversity* 21 (5). https://doi.org/10.1080/17550874.2019.1641757.

Schlossberg, Josh. 2014. "Wildfire Prevention or Forest Destruction?" *Boulder Weekly*, November 13, 25. https://www.boulderweekly.com/boulderganic/wildfire-prevention-or-forest-destruction/.

Schoennagel, Tania. 2017. "Adapt to More Wildfire in Western North American Forests as Climate Changes." *PNAS* 114 (18). https://doi.org/10.1073/pnas.1617464114.
Schoennagel, Tania, Thomas T. Veblen, and William H. Romme. 2004. "The Interaction of Fire, Fuels, and Climate across Rocky Mountain Forests." *BioScience* 54, no. 7(2004): 661–676.
Scientific American. 2012. "Is the Federal Government's $100-Million Predator Control Program in Need of Reform?" https://www.scientificamerican.com/article/federal-governments-predator-control-program/#:~:text=While%20the%20program%20does%20much,livestock%20does%20take%20up%20%24100.
Siirila-Woodburn, Erica, Alan Rhoades, Benjamin Hatchett, Laurie Huning, Julia Szinai, Christina Tague, Peter Nico, Daniel Feldman, Andrew Jones, William Collins, and Laurna Kaatz. 2021. "A Low-to-No Snow Future and Its Impacts on Water Resources in the Western United States." *Nature* 2 (November). https://doi.org/10.1038/s43017-021-00219-y.
Simard, Suzanne. 2021. *Finding the Mother Tree: Discovering the Wisdom of the Forest.* 2021. New York: Alfred Knopf Publishing. (Much more than covering mycorrhizal fungi, the book truly shows how complexity leads to resilience and how modern logging and climate change are threatening forest resilience.)
Smith, David. 1986. *Ouray, Chief of the Utes.* Ouray, CO: Wayfinder Press Publishing.
Soulé, Michael, and Reed Noss. 1998. "Rewilding and Biodiversity: Complementary Goals for Continental Conservation." *Wild Earth.* https://rewilding.org/wp-content/uploads/2012/04/RewildingBiod.pdf.
State of Colorado. 2022. *Colorado Population.* Accessed October 16, 2023. https://worldpopulationreview.com/states/colorado-population.
State of Colorado Greenhouse Gas Reduction Roadmap. 2021. https://drive.google.com/file/d/1jzLvFcrDryhhs9ZkT_UXkQM_0LiiYZfq/view.
Stevens-Rumann, Camille, Kerry B. Kemp, Philip E. Higuera, Brian J. Harvey, Monica T. Rother, Daniel C. Donato, Penelope Morgan, and Thomas T. Veblen. 2018. "Evidence for Declining Forest Resilience to Wildfires under Climate Change." *Ecology Letters.* 21:243–252. https://doi.org/10.1111/ele.12889.
Touma, Danielle, Samantha Stevenson, Daniel L. Swain, Deepti Singh, Dmitra Kalashnikov, and Xinying Huang. 2022. "Climate Change Increases Risk of Extreme Rainfall following Wildfire in the Western United States." *Science Advances* 8 (13). https://doi.org/10.1126/sciadv.abm0320.
US Forest Service. n.d.a. "Engelmann Spruce." https://www.srs.fs.usda.gov/pubs/misc/ag_654/volume_1/picea/engelmannii.htm#:~:text=Engelmann%20spruce%20grows%20in%20a,C%20(90%C2%B0%20F).
US Forest Service. n.d.b. "Forest Health" definition. https://www.fs.usda.gov/science-technology/forest-health#:~:text=Forest%20health%20has%20been%20defined,lead%20to%20sustainable%20ecological%20conditions.
US Forest Service. n.d.c. "Our History." https://www.fs.usda.gov/learn/our-history.

US House of Representatives: Document Repository. 2021. "Open Letter to President Biden and Members of Congress from Scientists: It Is Essential to Remove Climate-Harming Logging and Fossil Fuel Provisions from Reconciliation and Infrastructure Bills." November 4. https://docs.house.gov/meetings/GO/GO28/20220316/114492/HHRG-117-GO28-Wstate-KingC-20220316-SD004.pdf.

Veblen, T. T., W. H. Romme, and C. Regan. 2012. "Regional Application of Historical Ecology at Ecologically Defined Scales: Forest Ecosystems in the Colorado Front Range." Chapter 10 in *Historical Environmental Variation in Conservation and Natural Resource Management*, edited by J. A. Wiens, G. D. Hayward, H. D. Safford, and Catherine Giffen, 149–165. Wiley-Blackwell. https://doi.org/10.1002/9781118329726.

Welch, Craig. 2023. "Seasons Out of Synch." *National Geographic* (Washington, DC), May 14.

Wiles, Tay. 2016. "Malheur Occupation, Explained." https://www.hcn.org/articles/oregon-occupation-at-wildlife-refuge.

Williams, A. Park, Benjamin I. Cook, and Jason E. Smerdon. 2022. "Rapid Intensification of the Emerging Southwestern North American Megadrought in 2020–2021." *Nature Climate Change* 12:232–234. https://doi.org/10.1038/s41558-022-01290-z.

Williams, A. Park, Ben Cook, et al., 2020. "Large Contribution to Anthropogenic Warming to an Emerging North American Megadrought." *Science*. https://doi.org/10.1126/science.aaz9600.

Williams, Florence. 2020. *The Nature Fix*. New York: W. W. Norton and Company. (A fascinating look at how visits to forests improve our health. I am in total agreement.)

Woelders, Lineke, Jeff Lukas, Liz Payton, and Benét Duncan. 2020. *Snowpack Monitoring in the Rocky Mountain West: A User Guide*. Boulder: Western Water Assessment, University of Colorado.

World Meteorological Society. 2023. "July 2023 Is Set to Be the Hottest Month on Record." https://public.wmo.int/en/media/press-release/july-2023-set-be-hottest-month-record.

Xiao, Mu, Bradley Udall, and Dennis P. Lettenmaier. 2018. "On the Causes of Declining Colorado River Streamflows." *Water Resources Research* 54 (9). https://doi.org/10.1029/2018WR023153.

Yochim, Michael. 2022. *Requiem for America's Best Idea: National Parks in the Era of Climate Change*. Albuquerque: University of New Mexico Press.

Zwinger, Ann, and Beatrice Willard. 1972. *Land above the Trees*. New York: Harper and Row.

Index

Abbey, Ed, 56
acid mine drainage, 37, 89
Adams, Rick, 42
agriculture, water for, 29, 97
Alder Creek, 81
Alferd Packer Massacre Site, 94
algae: green, 31; snow, 31
Aloha Lake, 104
Along the Colorado Trail (Fielder), 109
alpine avens, 90
alpine forget-me-nots, 90
alpine soils, permafrost and, 27
Alpine Tunnel, 40, 67
alpine zones, 25, 90–91
Amanita muscaria, 113
Amax, 32
American Basin, 96
Amethyst (town), 88
Amethyst mine, 88
Andrus, Robert, 43–44, 84

Animas Canyon, 85, 108
Animas River, 96, 100, 103, 105, 107, 108, 115; spill in, 89
Animas Valley, 107, 114, 115
Anne, 20, 25, 30, 37, 38, 47, 88, 90, 107
Ant Creek, 75
Appalachian Trail (AT), 6, 127
Arapaho-Roosevelt National Forest, 29, 41
Arapahos, 4, 65
Arkansas River, 34, 35, 37, 62, 63
arnicas, 68
aspen, 25, 30, 34, 45, 102, 119
AT. *See* Appalachian Trail
avalanches, 26, 27, 32

backpacking, 20, 59, 61, 65, 104, 108
Baker's Park, 107
bats, climate change and, 42
Battaglia, Mike, 13
Bear Lake, 47

bears, 14; black, 77, 103, 119, 120; grizzly, 28, 101, 102
Beartown, 105
beaver ponds, 21, 22
beavers, 21, 103, 119; as keystone species, 22
bees, 75–79
beetles, 118; bark, 29, 44, 52, 83, 84, 85; dead forest and, 82–89; pine, 29, 30, 120; spruce, 82, 84, 85, 120
Benedict, Audrey, 10
Bennet, Michael, 110, 125
Bent's Fort, 81
Biden, Joseph, 121, 124, 136; Camp Hale and, 34; renewable energy and, 125
Big Meadows, 47
Big Oil, 135
bighorn sheep, 9, 14, 41, 77, 91, 100, 120; decline of, 119; managing, 93–94; watching, 76
biodiversity, 3, 22, 23, 44, 58, 75–79, 96, 105, 120, 121; increase in, 118; mammal, 119; protecting, 126
biomarkers, identifying, 70
biotic communities, 117
Bird Conservancy of the Rockies, 42
birds: climate change and, 42; losses of, 42; migratory, 28; populations of, 120
bison, 75–79
Bison Peak, 68
Black Americans, vote for, 66
Black Canyon, 82
Black Creek, 22
Black Elk, x
Black Forest Fire, 43
Black Lives Matter, 37
Blackhawk Pass, 112
BLM. *See* Bureau of Land Management
blood pressure, 128
blood snow, 31
Blue River Valley, 30, 31, 32
bobcats, 27, 77, 80
Bolam Pass, 112
Boletus rubriceps, 113
boreholes, 85
Boss Lake, 40
Boulder County, wildfires in, 50
Breckenridge, 29, 30, 31

Brian the Bishop (Litebrite), 92, 99, 100, 108, 127
bristlecone pine, 25, 30, 118
Brooks Lake, 101
brown creepers, 22
brown-capped rosy finch, 42
Brunot Agreement (1873), 107, 116
Buffalo Creek, 21, 52
Buffalo Creek Fire, 16–20; burn scar of, 16; rain following, 52
Buffalo Creek Road, 20
Build Back Better, 125
bumblebees, 78
Bundy, Ammon, 72
Bureau of Land Management (BLM), 5, 23, 37, 54, 55, 57, 58, 71, 72, 122, 124; cattle regulation and, 73; politics with, 56
Bureau of Livestock and Mining, 56
Bureau of Reclamation, 36
burn scars, xii, 16, 45
buttercups, 78
butterflies, 75–79, 91, 114; monarch, 79

cable media, 116
Cache la Poudre River, 52
Cameron Peak, 41
Cameron Peak Fire, 46, 52
campfires, 45, 59, 124
Camp Hale, 33, 34
Camp Hale–Continental Divide National Monument, 34, 125
Camp Hale Wilderness, 58
Cannings, Syd, 78
carbon dioxide, 8, 73, 124, 132; emissions, 122; equivalents, 53; sequestered, 52, 84
carbon footprint (CF), 53, 127, 131, 132; cattle and, 73; reducing, 59, 124, 133
carbon offsets, 59, 127
carbon storage, 93
carbon taxes, 123
Carla, 108, 111, 112, 115, 116
Carlton Tunnel, 36
Carpenter Peak, 9
Carson (town), 98
Carson Peak, 96
Carson Peak Roadless Area, 96

Index

Carson Saddle, 98, 112
Cascade Creek, 111, 112
Cataract Creek, 33
cattle, 75, 76, 102; carbon footprint and, 73; removing, 73
cattle grazing, 55, 74, 126; regulating, 73
CDT. *See* Continental Divide Trail
Cebolla Creek, 80
Central San Juan bighorn metapopulation, 93
CF. *See* carbon footprint
Chaffee County, 62
Chalk Creek, 40
Chalk Creek Pass, 40
Chambers, Marin, 19
chemical hazards, 89
Cheyenne (city), 65, 67
Cheyennes, 4
chickadees, 22
chiming bells, 68
Chiodi, Andrew, 17
Chipeta, 64, 66, 127
Chivington, John, 4
Chlamydomonas nivalis, 31
civil rights, 116
Clark's nutcrackers, 15, 16
Clear Creek, South Fork of, 38
climate change, ix, xi, 3, 14, 33, 49, 51, 52, 58, 76, 78, 79, 86, 87; adapting to, 22, 118, 120; anthropogenic, 19, 20, 96; bats and, 42; beef consumption and, 73; birds and, 42; concerns about, 9, 12, 72; defining, 117; drought and, 19, 22, 106; era of, 6; fighting, 22, 53, 59; forest mortality and, 83; impact of, 23, 27, 117, 120; migration and, 23; national parks and, 57; as national security risk, 8; plant/animal community and, 77; recovery and, 73; reducing, 123; slow-motion, 8; snowpack and, 35, 51; temperatures and, 106; tree regeneration and, 14; vulnerability to, 105; weather/climate and, 8; wildfires and, 20, 43
climate conditions, 16, 18, 44
climate corridors, 76
climate warming, 44, 71, 84; permafrost melting and, 26
climate zones, 90–91

Cochetopa, defined, 68, 76
Cochetopa Creek, 75
Cochetopa Hills, 68, 75, 76, 107
Cochetopa Park, 74
Cochetopa Pass, 68, 73, 74, 81, 82
Cochetopa Valley, 11, 61, 68, 75
cold air pools (CAPS), 21–22
Collegiate Peaks, 38, 39
Collegiate Peaks Wilderness, 38
Collegiate West Traverse, 38–41
Colorado Bird Observatory, 42
Colorado Climate Center, 43–44
Colorado Climate Plan, 132, 133
Colorado Forest Restoration Institute, 19
Colorado Fourteeners Initiative, 31
Colorado Midland Railway, 34, 36
Colorado Mountain Club, 5, 58, 61, 62, 75; Wilderness School of, 20
Colorado Natural Heritage Program, 10, 105, 119
Colorado Outdoor Recreation and Economy Act, 110
Colorado Parks and Wildlife, 34, 35, 48, 58, 76, 81, 101, 102; black bears/mountain lions and, 103
Colorado Public Radio, 72
Colorado River, 96, 100, 105; Water Conservation District, 97; water shortage on, 97
Colorado State Forest Service, 84, 112, 122
Colorado State University, 19, 47
Colorado Trail (CT): coronavirus confinement and, 9; ecology of, 128; hiking, 3–7, 80; inspiration from, 117; map of, viiif; Western Slope of, 15
Colorado Trail Databook, The, 6
Colorado Trail Foundation (CTF), 5, 6, 40, 62, 75, 127, 128; mission/vision of, 126
columbines, 68, 114
Commodore mine, 88
Coney Summit, 98
conifers, 5, 10, 12, 13, 16, 18, 27, 28, 30, 87, 119; bark beetles and, 29; regeneration of, 44, 49
ConocoPhillips, 99
Continental Divide, 11, 23, 30, 33, 35, 36, 41, 47, 58, 61, 64, 67, 68, 79, 81, 105

Continental Divide Trail (CDT), 3, 6, 7, 24, 28, 29, 76, 96, 101, 104, 105, 118, 127
Cook, Benjamin, 44
Copper Mountain, 32
corn lilies, 114
Cottonwood Pass, 39
cottonwoods, 10
Covid-19 pandemic, 49, 71; beginnings of, 8–12; deaths from, 142; politics and, 117; stressors, 70
coyotes, 27, 77, 119
Creede, 66, 79, 80, 87, 90, 94; mining in, 88, 89
Creede, Nicholas C., 88
Crested Butte, 78
CT. *See* Colorado Trail
CTF. *See* Colorado Trail Foundation
culture wars, 6

Davis, Kimberley, 18
Dawes Allotment, 103
debris flows, 52
deer, 28, 32, 77, 102, 119, 120; mule, 14, 76, 103
Deer Creek, 113
Delta, 72
dendrochronology, 13
Denver, John, 98
Denver and Rio Grande Railroad Company, 115
Denver and Rio Grande Western Railroad, 34, 62, 67, 94, 108
Denver, South Park and Pacific Railroad, 9, 67
Denver Water Board, 16, 32
Department of Game, Fish and Forestry, 68
Desert Land Act (1877), 55
Dillon, 32
Dillon Reservoir, 30, 31, 32
disturbance regimes, 14
diversity, 78, 112; animal, 91; genetic, 76
Domínguez, Atanasio, 115
Domíguez-Escalante expedition, 115
Domke, Grant, 52
Douglas fir, 4, 10, 12, 13, 14, 15, 18, 19, 45, 76, 119
Douglas, Margaret R., 78

drought, 8, 14, 15, 16, 29, 42, 45, 46, 68, 71, 83, 84, 96, 103, 112, 118, 135; climate change and, 19, 22, 106; extreme/exceptional, 43; SAD and, 106; stress from, 85; west-side, 44
drying conditions, impact of, 53
Dunne, K. A., 97
Durango, 3, 5, 12, 69, 85, 106, 108, 114, 115, 116
Durango Herald, 92
Durango and Silverton Narrow Gauge Railroad, 105, 106, 107–8

Eagle County, 35
Eagle River, 33
eagles, 65, 119
Eagle Valley Clean Energy, 31
Earth Day, 125
earthflow, 98
East Creede, 88
East Troublesome Creek Fire, 41, 46, 47, 118
ecological change, 15, 50, 119
ecological traps, 101
ecosystems, 5, 9, 43, 47, 50–53, 83, 87, 99, 118, 119, 131; alpine tundra, 86; complexity of, 128; future of, 120; global warming and, 78; health of, 58, 76; mountain, 7, 28, 73; resilience of, 120; restoring, 44, 121; sustainable, 50; tree encroachment in, 91; woodland, 10
ectomycorrhizal fungi, 12, 18
Eddiesville trailhead, 80
education: embracing, 126; environmental, 5, 126
El Diente Peak, 112
El Dorado Lake, 105
electric vehicles, 132, 136
elephantellas, 78
elk, 14, 28, 41, 76, 77, 91, 100, 102, 103, 119, 120; culling, 48; overgrazing by, 48; population of, 47–48, 57; transplanting, 47
Elk Creek, 105
Elk Park, 105
Elk Ridge, 33
Endangered Species Act, 119
Engineer Mountain, 85

environmental issues, ix, 7, 24, 46, 126, 127; mining and, 89
Environmental Protection Agency (EPA), 16, 89, 132
Equity Mine, 87
erosion, 49, 52, 57, 91
erythronium grandiflorum, 79
Escalante, Silvestre Vélez de, 115
Estes Park, evacuation of, 47
Evans, John, 4, 32
evaporation, 45, 51, 99

FarOut phone app, 6
Federal Land Policy and Management Act (1976), 56
Fielder, John, 108–9
Fielder, JT, 108–9
Finding the Mother Tree (Simard), 11
fire bans, 7, 13
firebrands, 46
fire-industrial complex, 123
fire regimes, 18, 46, 118
Fish Canyon Tuff, 80
fishing, 9, 16, 48
Flagler Rock, 114
Flattop Mountain, 47
Flint Lakes Area, 104
flooding, ix, 22, 85, 94, 96, 125; flash, 50, 52, 63
food: chain, 103; hiking, 63–64; shortages, 135
Ford, Robert, 88
Ford, Ryan, 103–4
Forest Action Plan, 122
forest bathing, 70
forest fires, 13–16
forest health, 46, 50, 126
forest management, 52, 122
forest plans, 23, 126
Fort Duchesne, 107
Fort Lyon, 4
fossil fuels, 53, 98, 121, 125, 136
Fountain in the Sky, 96–98
416 Fire, 114
foxes, 27
Franklin, Ben, xi
Frémont, John C., 25, 81, 82
Frisco, 31, 122

Front Range, 13, 18, 26, 31, 36, 41, 47, 86, 103
Frosty, 61, 62, 63, 68, 69, 73, 74, 75, 85, 87, 92, 95, 98, 106, 108, 127, fig. 1; illness for, 110–13
fuels reduction, 31, 83, 121
Fuels Reduction Project, 31

Gambel oak, 12, 15, 115, 119
Gaskill, Gundrun "Gudy," 5, 115
General Land Office, 54, 56
General Mining Law (1872), 55
Georgia Pass, 29
GHG. *See* greenhouse gases
Ghost Grizzlies (Petersen), 101
glacier lily, 79, 86, 105
Glacier National Park, 57, 101
glaciers, 26, 39, 42, 85
Glasgow Climate Conference, 124
Glenwood Canyon, 52
global warming, 87, 93, 122; ecosystems and, 78
globeflowers, 28, 86
goats, 31; mountain, 27
Godey, Alexis, 82
gold, mining for, 115–16
Gold Hill, 30
Gold King spill (2005), 89
Gold Rush (1858), 4
gophers, 27; pocket, 85
Gore Range, 33
Grand Canyon National Park, 57
Grand Junction, 72
Grand Lake, 46, 47
Grant, Ulysses S.: Ouray and, 66
Grasshopper, 33, 36, 37, 38, 41, 61, 62, 63, 67, 68, 69, 73–74, 75, 85, 99, 100, 108, 111, 112, 115, 116, 127, fig. 1; hiking with, 24–30, 90–96
grasslands, 15, 68, 73, 95, 118, 119, 123; burning, 49
Grays Peak, 31, 32
grazing, 56, 92, 93, 95; allotments, 72, 73; cattle, 55, 73, 74, 126; livestock, 58, 73, 119; rotational, 73. *See also* overgrazing
Great Spirit, x, xi
green space, health benefits of, 71
Greenhorn Mountains, 47
Greenhouse Gas Reduction Roadmap, 124

greenhouse gases (GHG), xii, 53, 120, 131, 132, 136; emissions of, 73, 98, 127; reducing, 8, 37, 123
Grenadier Mountains, 85
Grizzly Creek Fire, mudslides/debris flows from, 52
groundwater, recharging, 35, 51, 98, 99
grouse, 14; blue/dusky, 87; sage, 28, 74
Guardian, The, 99
Gudy's Rest, 115, fig. 9
Guller Creek, 32
Gulliford, Andrew, 92–93
Gunnison, 72, 102
Gunnison, John, 82
Gunnison River, 96; Lake Fork of, 98
Gunnison Valley, 68, 72
Gypsum, 31

habitats, 29, 45, 49, 52, 74, 76, 86, 102, 119, 120, 121, 126; alpine, 42; altering, 77; grizzly, 101; loss, 78, 79, 81, 103; lynx, 80–81; transformation of, 47; wetland, 22, 35; wildlife, 4, 47, 118
Hagerman Trestle, 36
Hagerman Tunnel, 36
Halfmoon Creek, 37
hallucinogens, 113
Hancock (town), 40
Hancock Lakes, 40
Handies Peak, 96
Handlebars, 106
Hardin, Garrett, xi
Hart, Sarah J., 84
Hayden, Ferdinand, 34–35
Hayes, Mark, 42
Hayes, Rutherford B.: Ouray and, 66
Hayhoe, Katharine, 53
Hayman Fire, 14, 16–20, 41, 43, 119; burn scar of, 16
herbicides, 79
herbivores, 103
Hermosa Creek, 112, 113
Hermosa Peak, 112
Hermosa Special Management Area, 112, 125
Hermosa Wilderness, 58
Hi Meadow Fire, 16

High Country News, 108
high-stand densities, causes of, 13–14
Hinsdale County, 100
History Colorado, 109
Holy Cross Wilderness, 34
Holy Moses mine, 88
Holy Springs Wilderness, 58
Homestake mine, 89
Homestake Water Project, 35
Homestead Act (1862), 55
Homo sapiens, land ethic and, xi
Hope Mountain, 38
Hope Pass, 38
humidity, relative, 7, 17
hummingbirds, 28, 77, 78, 91
hummocks, 27
Hunchback Pass, 105
Hunt Lake, 41
hunting, 57, 75, 81, 119, 124; buffalo, 4; sport, 102; trophy, 48
Huron Peak, 38
hurricanes, ix, 49, 135
hydroelectric power, 29
hydrology, 36, 53, 87
hydrophobic soils, 18, 52
hypothermia, 88, 90, 92

Ice Lake Fire, 124
Ice Lakes Basin, 111
Ice Mountain, 39
Idaho Springs, 47
Ignacio (town), 66, 103
Ignacio, Chief, 103
Independence Pass Road, 37
Indian Ridge, 113–16
Indian Trail Ridge, 114
Inflation Reduction Act (2022), 125
Inouye, David, 78
insecticides, 79
insects, 19, 43, 83, 103, 114, 118
Intergovernmental Panel on Climate Change (IPCC), 87, 132

Jackson, William Henry, 34, 35
James, Jesse, 88
Janet's Cabin, 33

Janousek, William M., 78
Jarosa Mesa, 95
Jefferson Creek, 25
Jimtown, 88
John Muir Trail, 24, 63
Junction Creek, 115, fig. 9; bridge, 114
Junction Creek Canyon, 115
Junction Creek Drainage, 15
juniper, 72, 119; rocky mountain, 10

Kauffman, Boone, 122
Kawaneeche Visitor Center, 49
Kearny, Stephen W., 81
Kennebec Pass, 114
Kenosha Mountains, 21
Kenosha Pass, 4, 20, 23, 24, 25
Kentucky Belle mine, 88
Ketcham, Christopher, 73, 119
King Boletes, 113
King, Martin Luther, Jr., 66
Kip's Grill, 88
Kite Lake, 105
Kokomon Pass, 33
Koshare Kiva, 65
krummholz, 91

La Garita Caldera, 79, 80
La Garita Peak, 80
La Garita Stock Driveway, 95
La Garita Wilderness, 75, 79–82, fig. 3
Lake Ann, 39
Lake Ann Pass, 39
Lake Baldy, 69
Lake City, 66, 80, 85, 94–95
Lake Dillon, 32
Lake San Cristobal, 98
Lakes Basin, 110
Lakotas, x, 65, 71
Lame Deer, x
Lamont Doherty Earth Observatory, 44
Land Above the Trees (Zwinger and Willard), 91
land managers, 57, 59, 89, 121
land use disturbance, 51
Lands and Minerals operations, 56
landscape, 5; headwater, ix; mountain, ix, xii; transforming, 66

Landscapes, reprint from, 131–33
Larkin, Narasimhan K., 17
Last Chance mine, 88
Leadville, 34, 37, 66, 103
Leave No Trace (LNT), 45, 58, 124, 126, 127, 131
Leopold, Aldo, x–xi, 117
Lettenmaier, Dennis P., 97
life zones, 10, 11, 30, 115
Light, William Sidney "Cap," 88
light intensity, 45
lightning storms, 39, 40, 90, 92
limber pine, 25, 30, 76, 118
Lime Creek Drainage, 111
Lime Creek wildfire, 111
Lincoln, Abraham: Ouray and, 66
Little Cataract Lake, 98
Little Scraggy Mountain, 20
livestock: GHG and, 73; grazing, 58, 73, 119; mountain lions and, 102; wolves and, 102
Lizard Head, 112
llamas, 20, 108–9
LNT. *See* Leave No Trace
lodgepole forests, 34, 46, 118–19
lodgepole pine, 10, 12, 18, 25, 29–30, 36, 45, 71, 76; regeneration by, 48–49
logging, 11, 13, 56, 121–22
Los Piños, 75, 80
Los Piños Agency, 75
Lost Creek, North Fork of, 21, 22
Lost Creek Wilderness, 20–23, 68
Lost Gulch trailhead, 22
Louis IX, 80
Louisville, 49; fire in, 123, 124, 135
low-to-no snow, predicting, 98
Lucas, Bill, 5
Lujan Forest Road, 71
lupines, 105
lynx, 27, 77, 101, 119, 120; snowshoe hare and, 80–81; as threatened species, 80

Malheur National Wildlife Refuge, 72
mammal ranges, shifts in, 86
Manchin, Joe, 125
marmots, 91
marsh marigolds, 86

Marshall Fire, 49, 123
Marshall Pass, 64, 67, 75
Marston, Ed: death of, 108
mass extinction, 96
Masterson, Bat, 88
Mattson, Dave, 101
McCain, Christy, 86
Meeker, Nathan, 107
Meeker Massacre (1879), 66, 107, 116
megadroughts, 44, 73, 97, 117
megafires, 17, 49, 83, 84, 118, 123; fear of, 41; frequency of, 43; impact of, 52
Merrill, Troy, 101
methane, 8, 73, 132
migrations, 22, 42, 77; climate change and, 23; plant/animal, 91
Millennium Ecosystem Assessment, 50
Million Dollar Highway, 116
Milly, P. C. D., 97
Mineral County, 88, 89
mining, 23, 40, 56, 66, 88, 108, 110, 115; camps, 4; environmental damage by, 89; hard rock, 89; placer, 62; waste from, 37
Mississippi River, 37, 55
mitigation, 121, 123; wildfire, 115
Molas Pass, 26, 105, 110, 111
molybdenum, 32
Monarch Crest, 41, 61, 64, 126
Monarch Pass, 24, 62, 63, 71, 116; forest mortality and, 82; trailhead, fig. 1
Monarch Ski Area, 41
Monarch Spur RV Park and Campground, 63
monkey flowers, 99
monkshoods, 78
monsoons, 39, 40, 68, 90, 98–100
Montrose, 66, 75
moose, 21, 27, 32, 33, 38, 49, 75, 77, 103, 119, 120, fig. 3
Morrey, Gabi, 12
mortality, 42, 80; drought, 84; forest, 15, 43, 71, 82, 83, 84, 118; insect, 53, 119; pine beetle, 30; rates, 44; rise of, 44; seedling, 83; spruce-beetle-caused, 84; tree, 44, 84, 122
Mosquito Range, 23
mosquitos, 25, 67, 78, 108

Motagnard Tribes, 69
moths, 77; Police Car, 114
mountain lions, 77, 119, 120; hunting, 102; killing, 103; livestock and, 102
mountain mahogany, 15, 119
Mountain Studies Institute, 87
mountain traverse, fig. 4
Mountain Utes, 4, 66, 75
Mount Blue Sky, 32
Mount Chipeta, 64
Mount Columbia, 38
Mount Elbert, 31, 37
Mount Elbert Pumped Storage hydroelectric plant, 37
Mount Eolus, 85
Mount Evans, 32
Mount Guyot, 29
Mount Harvard, 38
Mount Kilimanjaro, 24
Mount Massive, 31, 36
Mount Massive Wilderness, 36
Mount of the Holy Cross, 34, 35
Mount Ouray, 64, 67
Mount Oxford, 38
Mount Princeton, 38
Mount Princeton Hot Springs, 40
Mount Saint Helens, 80
Mount Whitney, 37
Mount Wilson, 111
Mount Yale, 38, 39
mudslides, 49, 52
Mueller, Andy, 96
Muir, John, 71
mushrooms, psilocybin-containing, 113
Mycoplasma ovipenumoniae, 93
mycorrhizal fungi, 11, 30, 31, 112, 113

National Forest System, public domain lands in, 55
National Geographic, 79
National Interagency Fire Center, 17
National Oceanic and Atmospheric Administration (NOAA), 49
National Park Service (NPS), 55, 57, 122
National Park Service Organic Act (1916), 57
national parks, climate change and, 57

National Scenic Trail (CDT), 126
National Wilderness Preservation System, 56
National Wildland Fires Cohesive Strategy, 122
Native Americans, 82; public lands and, 54; vote for, 66
Natural Arch, 93
Natural Audubon Society, 42
natural climate, variability in, 20
Naturalist's Guide to the Southern Rockies (Benedict), 10
Nature Conservancy, 132
nature fix, 70–71
Nature Fix, The (Williams), 70
NCAR wildfire, 49
Needle Mountains, 85
nitrogen deposition, 93
Niwot Ridge, 26, 93
North American Monsoon, 40
North Creede, 88
North Fork Fire, 16
North Fork Valley, 16
North Park, 102
North Pass, 71, 73
Northern Cheyenne tribe, 4
Noss, Reid: rewilding and, 58
NPS. *See* National Park Service
nunataks, 85
nuthatches, 22

Obama, Barack, 15, 113
Odell, Dave, 104
Oglala Sioux, x
oil and gas drilling, 34, 56, 62, 74
O'Kelley, Ed, 88
Old Faithful, 24
old man of the mountain, 90
Olympic National Park, 57
Ophir Mountain Forest Health, 31
Ophir Project, 122
Orleans Club, 88
Ouray, 103, 116, 119, 127; Colorado population at time of, 66–67; land of, 61–70, 72; Tabeguache and, 64, 107
Ouray's Treaty (1868), 107
Outdoor Industry Association, 51

overcrowding, 37, 58, 67, 69
overgrazing, xi, xii, 15, 71, 72, 73, 95, 103, 119
Overlook Trail, 113
overpopulation, 11, 69, 103, 116
overwintering, 78, 79

Pacific Crest Trail (PCT), 6, 7, 104, 118, 127
paintbrushes, 68
Paiutes, 82
Palmer, William Jackson, 108
Paonia, 108
Paris Agreement, 125, 132, 133
Paris Climate Conference, 124
Pawnee montane skipper, 79
PCT. *See* Pacific Crest Trail
Pearson, Mark, 21, 100, 110
permafrost, 26–27
pesticides, using, 79
Petersen, David, 101
phenology, 77
pikas, 85–86, 87, 91
Pike National Forest, 9
Pike–San Isabel National Forest, forest plan for, 23
Pikes Peak, 61
Pinchot, Gifford, 55
Pine Creek Valley, 73
pine forests, burning, 49
Pine Gulch Fires, 41
pine martens, 27, 87
Pingree Park campus, 47
pink snow, 31
pinyon, 15, 72, 73, 119
pinyon-juniper woodland, 119
Platte River, 79
pneumonia, 92
Pole Creek, 99, 105, 106
Polis, Jared, 136
politics, 6, 24, 41, 56, 127, 133; climate change and, 53; Covid-19 pandemic and, 117; polarized, 116
pollination, 50, 77–78, 79, 83
pollution: air, 57, 58, 70, 93; carbon, 124; noise, 57, 70; plastic, xii; water, 57, 70
Ponderosa pine, 5, 10, 12, 13, 14, 18, 19, 29, 50, 76, 119

Pool Table Mesa, 82
porcupines, 14, 27
Porter's lovage, 113
postholing, 27
Potter, Brian E., 17
Powderhorn Wilderness, 80
precipitation, 9, 10, 45, 51, 52, 85, 86, 93, 119
predator control programs, 119
preservation, 34, 56, 57, 58, 59
Prichard, Susan, 121, 122
pronghorn antelope, 76
ptarmigan, 27, 91; white-tailed, 86–87
public land managers/ranchers, 120, 121
public lands, 71, 83, 104, 119; grazing on, 72, 95; history of, 54–56; legacy of, ix, 58; Native Americans and, 54; sheep/cattle raising on, 55, 73
Public Lands Foundation, 54
Pueblo, 36
Pueblo County, 47

rainfall, 40, 52, 85
ram's horns, 68
ravens, 27
Razor Creek, 69
recreation, 5, 34, 37, 50–51, 56, 57, 59, 69, 91, 126
red flag warnings, 7
Red Mountain, 99
Red Mountain Pass, 91
reforestation, 15, 16, 19, 31, 48, 83, 127
Refrigerator Gulch, 21
refugia, 22, 23, 44, 121, 126, 131, 135
regeneration, 11, 13, 18, 44, 48–49, 83, 111; climate change and, 14; forest, 19; natural, 15; spruce, 45, 84
renewable energy, 29, 125, 136
REPLANT Act, 125
Requiem for America's Best Idea: National Parks in the Era of Climate Change (Yochim), 57
resilience, 14, 50, 83, 120, 121; building, 122; challenging, 12
rewilding, 58
Reyher, Ken, 71, 72
Rhizopogon, 12
Ridgeway, 85

Rio Grande, 88, 96, 100, 105–6
Rio Grande National Forest, 82
Rio Grande Pyramid, 104
Rio Grande Reservoir, 103
riparian, 44, 76
roadless areas, 4, 33, 45, 57, 58, 96, 110, 122
Rock Creek trailhead, 22
Rockdale, 38
Rockström, Johan, xi
Rocky Mountain Biological Laboratory, 78
Rocky Mountain National Park, 26, 46, 47; elk in, 48
Rocky Mountain Restoration Initiative, 115
rodents, 27, 87
Rodman, Kyle, 14, 15, 84
"Rogue Agency, The" (Ketcham), 119
Rolling Mountain, 111
Rolling Rock trailhead, 21
Romme, William, 17
Roosevelt, Theodore, 55
Roxborough State Park, 9
Ruby Creek, 95
Ruess, Everett, 104
runoff, 51, 52, 97, 99, 120; early, 29; peak, 28; timing of, 96
Rusho, W. L., 104

sagebrush, 74, 119
sagebrush leks, 28
Sagebrush Rebellion, 58, 72
Salida, 66, 103; smelters in, 62–63
San Juan mining district, 107, 115
San Juan Mountains, 18, 27, 44, 68, 79, 80, 81, 85, 86, 92, 93, 100, 101, 102, 106, 115, 116, 124
San Juan Mountains Association, 12
San Juan National Forest, 82, 91
San Juan River, 100
San Juan Volcano, 79
San Luis Pass, 87, 92, 112
San Luis Peak, 26, 31, 61, 80, 93
San Luis Valley, 68, 81, 103
San Miguel Peak, 110
San Miguel Roadless Area, 110
Sand County Almanac, A (Leopold), xi, 117
Sand Creek, 4

Sand Creek Massacre, 32
Sargents Mesa, 69
Saving Us (Hayhoe), 53
Sawatch Range, 38, 68
scarlet gilias, 78
Schoennagel, Tania, 17, 122
Science, xi, 42, 97
scrub oak, 10, 12
Sea of Cortez, 100
sea level, rise of, 135
Searle Pass, 33
Second Los Piños Agency, 66
seedling, 11, 13, 14, 15, 16, 18, 19, 49, 83; development of, 45, 84
senecios, 68
Shavano Peak, 31, 41
sheep, 10, 95, 102; allotment, 94; grazing, 92, 93; raising, 55. *See also* bighorn sheep
Sheep Creek, 38
Sheep Mountain Special Management, 111
showy daisies, 68
shrubland, 15, 20, 73, 95, 118, 119
Sierra lilies, 105
Siirila-Woodburn, Erica, 97
silver, mining for, 115–16
Silverton, 66, 80, 82, 89, 100, 106–9, 111, 116; described, 107
Simard, Suzanne, 11
Sinema, Kyrsten, 125
sky pilots, 90
Sliderock Ridge, 112
Slumgullion Slide, 98
smelting, 34, 62–63, 89, 94, 116
Smith, Jefferson Randolph "Soapy," 88
Smoky the Bear campaign, 43
snowfall, 26, 27, 50, 85
snowfields, 26, 42
snowmelt, 51, 72, 77, 79, 86, 99; importance of, 28
Snow Mesa, 92, 94
snowpack, 25, 28, 72, 83, 84, 96, 97, 99, 118, 120; climate change and, 35, 51; ephemeral, 98; loss of, 135; melting of, 27; storing, 51
snowshoe hare, 27; lynx and, 80–81
snowshoeing, 27

social media, 53, 116
social tolerance, 101, 102
soil contamination, large-scale, 63
solar electricity, 132
solar radiation, 45, 97
Soldierstone Memorial, 69
solifluction, 26
solution aversion, 53
Soulé, Michael: rewilding and, 58
South Arkansas River, 63; Middle Fork of, 40
South Fork (town), 89
South Park, 23, 25
South Park and Pacific Railroad, 25, 40
South Platte River, 4, 9, 12, 16, 51, 52
South San Juan Mountains, 101, 102
Southern Rocky Mountains, 14, 17, 51, 86
Southern Ute Reservation, 103
Southern Utes, 103
Speed, fig. 1, fig. 5, fig. 10
spirituality, Native American, x
Spring Creek, 52
Spring Creek Fire, 43
Spring Creek Pass, 94, 105
spruce, 80, 82, 115; Colorado blue, 76; drought-/beetle-resistant, 71; Engelmann, 4, 5, 10, 15, 18, 25, 30, 33, 45, 76, fig. 8; growth of, 83; regeneration of, 45, 84
spruce-fir forests, 43, 46, 49, 82
squirrels, 15, 27; Abert, 12, 14, 22; golden-mantled ground, 86; pine, 22
Staley, Steve, 126
stand-replacing events, 18
sterilization programs, 58
Stevens-Rumann, Camille, 14
Stewart Peak, 80
Stock-Raising Homestead Act (1916), 55, 95
Stony Pass, 99, 112
Stony Pass Alternate, 100
Stony Pass Road, 100, 106
stream bank stabilization, 35
stream corridors, 22, 23
stream flows, 51, 83, 98, 136; reducing, 96
streams, xii; shading of, 96
stress hormones, 128
stressors, pandemic-related, 71

String Town, 88
Strontia Springs, 16
Strontia Springs Reservoir, 52
subalpine fir, 18, 30, 33, 76, 80, 119
subalpine forests, 10, 16, 18, 25, 83, 84, fig. 6, fig. 7
subnivean, 85
succession, 11, 30
sudden aspen decline (SAD), 106
sunflowers, 78, 114
Superfund sites, 89
Superior, 49; fire in, 123–24, 135
Swan River, 29

Tabeguache, 64, 66, 103, 107
Tabeguache Peak, 41
Table Mountain, 49
tall larkspurs, 68
tansy asters, 113, 114
Taos, 64, 82
Tarryall Mountains, 42
Taylor Grazing Act, 95
Taylor Lake, 113, 114
Telluride, 82
temperatures, 22, 45; changes in, 9, 106; increase in, 87; stream, 105
Tenmile Creek Valley, 32
Tenmile Range, 30–31, 34
Tennessee Pass, 34
Tenth Mountain Division, 33, 34
Tenth Mountain Division Hut Association, 33
Texas Creek, 39
thawing, soil slumping from, 26
30×30 Initiative, 126
Thousand Island Lake, 104
Three Apostles, 39
thunderstorms, 39, 40, 90
Timber and Stone Act (1878), 55
Timber Culture Act (1873), 55
Tincup Basin, 112
Torreys Peak, 31
Touma, Danielle, 52
tourism, 50, 57, 89
Towaoc, 103
trail magic, UFOs and, 71–75

transpiration, 45, 51
Treaty of 1868, 64, 107, 116
tree density, 118
tree encroachment, 91
Treeline Restaurant, 37
Triple Crown Hiking Adventures (Ford), 6, 58
trophic cascades, 103
trout, xii, 41; brook, 21, 96; cutthroat, 96, 105, 120; rainbow, 96
tundra, 4, 11, 91, 99, 102
Turquoise Lake, 35, 36
Twin Lakes, 25, 37, 38, 40
Twin Sisters, 111
Two Forks, 16

Udall, Bradley, 97
UFOs, trail magic and, 71–75
Uinta chipmunk, 86
Uncompahgre River, 66, 75
Uncompahgre Wilderness, 80
United Nations, assessment by, 50
United Nations Food and Agricultural Organization, 73
United States Geological Survey (USGS), 124
University of Colorado Boulder, 14, 70, 84, 108
Upper Animas Valley, 107
Upper Arkansas Valley, 34, 41, 103
Upper Rio Grande Valley, 88
Upper Tonahutu Creek, 47
US Department of Agriculture, 55, 122; Wildlife Services program of, 119
US Department of Defense, climate change and, 8
US Department of the Interior, 55, 122
US Department of the Treasury, 54–55
US Fish and Wildlife Service, 34, 57
US Forest Service, 4, 5, 13, 22, 31, 45, 50, 55, 56, 72, 83, 91, 92, 94, 110, 114, 122; annual budget for, 123; climate change and, 127; land management by, 57; reroute by, 75; sheep management and, 93; Smoky the Bear and, 43
US Geological Survey, 34–35
US Grazing Service, 56
Ute Lake, 105

Ute Mountain Utes, 14, 100, 103, 107
Ute Reservation, 107
Utes, x, 4, 68, 75, 76, 103, 107, 127; burns by, 72; CT and, 54; silver/gold discoveries and, 115–16; Tabeguache/Uncompahgre band of, 64, 66

Valley of the Green River, 81
Valley of Lake Creek, 38
vapor pressure deficit (VPD), 17
Veblen, Tom, 15, 16, 17, 44, 71, 84, 118, 119, 121; fire suppression and, 18
Vestal Peak, 99
voles, 27, 85, 91

Wakan Tanka, x, xii
Waldo Canyon Fire, 43
Walker, Jerry Jeff, 62
Walker Ranch, 14
Walker Ranch Fire, 14, 20
Wannamaker Creek, 82
warming conditions, 22, 53, 119, 120
water resources, 35, 51, 97
water utilities, 8
watermelon snow, 31
watersheds, ix, 120
Waterton, 4, 12
Waterton Canyon, 3, 4, 9, 10
weasels, 87
Weminuche Creek, 104
Weminuche Pass, 104
Weminuche Wilderness, 58, 82, 85, 92, 99, 100–106; bighorn population, 93; elk herds in, 100
West Nile virus, 108
Western Slope, 11, 15, 36, 61, 100, 102; wilderness areas on, 110
Western spruce budworms, 82
Western Water Assessment, 51
Weston Pass, 23
wet meadowlands, 11, 35, 38, 74
wetlands, 22, 35, 44
Wheeler Geologic Area, 79
White Buffalo Calf Woman, x
White River Agency, 107
White River National Forest, 31

White River Utes, 66
White River War (1879), 66
Wild Connections, 21, 22–23, 42, 121, 132
wilderness, 4, 21, 35, 39, 41, 68, 120, 126; areas, 57, 58, 110; boundary, 36; defining, 57; designated, 75; high peaks, 36–37; protection, 21, 100; risks for, 45; twenty-first century, 56–59
Wilderness Act (1964), 21, 57, 79
Wilderness Trekking School, 14
wildfire zones, human habitation in, 122
wildfires, 7, 22, 25, 29, 35, 38, 41–45, 83, 96, 97, 111, 121, 135; carbon dioxide emissions and, 122; climate change and, 20, 40, 43; danger of, 11, 13, 46–50, 53, 122; extent of, 119; habitat transformation by, 47; as natural process, 118; nonforests after, 15; outbreaks of, 16; preventing/reducing, 31, 43, 115, 122, 123; rating, 17–18; severity of, 83
wildflowers, 25, 28, 30, 68, 76, 77, 78, 79, 86, 90, 99, 105, 110, 111, 113
wild horses, 58
wildland-urban interface (WUI), 49, 102, 121, 122, 123, 124, 135
wildlife, 103, 111, 118, 128; flourishing of, 126; losses of, 120; managing, 57; restoring, 120; watching, 76
wildlife managers, x, 47
Wildlife Services program (USDA), 119
Willard, Beatrice, 91
Williams, A. Park, 44
Williams, Old Bill, 81–82
Willis Creek, 38
Willow Project, 124
willows, 11, 22, 27, 33, 38, 39, 86, 87, 90, 93, 95, 98
Wilson Peak, 111–12
Wind River Indian Reservation, 65
Wind River Range, 28
Windom Peak, 85
"Window," 104
Windy Peak, 68
Wolf Creek Pass, 82
Wolf Restoration and Management Plan, 102

wolverines, 81, 101, 119, 120
wolves, 27, 48, 103, 119, 120; gray, 101, 102; introduction of, 100, 102; livestock and, 102; social tolerance of, 102
woodpeckers, 22
woolly thistle, 90
World Meteorological Society, 117
WUI. *See* wildland-urban interface

Xiao, Mu, 97

Yellowstone National Park, 57, 101
Yochim, Michael, 57
Yosemite National Park, 57
Yosemite Valley, 21

Zwinger, Ann, 91

About the Author

Karl Ford is a Triple Crowner, having completed America's three long trails, and has two completions of the Colorado Trail. He is author of *Triple Crown Hiking Adventures*. Karl holds a PhD from Colorado State University and is a retired environmental scientist and naturalist. He worked for the Bureau of Land Management in ecoregional assessment, climate change, and other natural resource sciences. He is a wilderness instructor for the Colorado Mountain Club and served on the Board of Wild Connections, a conservation nonprofit in Colorado. He dabbles in science education by college teaching, climate writing, and serving twenty-five years as a judge captain at the Colorado State Science and Engineering Fair. He has written for *Appalachian Journeys, Park Science, Colorado Central Magazine, ALDHA-West Gazette, Mile High Mountaineer*, and *Landscapes*. He can be found hiking anywhere there is wild nature.

www.ingramcontent.com/pod-product-compliance
Lightning Source LLC
Chambersburg PA
CBHW060607080526
44585CB00013B/713